FAMILY
IN
SOUTH
GLOUCESTERSHIRE
FOREST, VALE AND WOLD

Gordon Ottewell

Scarthin Books, Cromford, Derbyshire   1990

FAMILY WALKS
IN SOUTH GLOUCESTERSHIRE

Family Walks Series
General Editor: Norman Taylor

THE COUNTRY CODE
Guard against all risk of fire
Fasten all gates
Keep dogs under proper control
Keep to paths across farm land
Avoid damaging fences, hedges and walls
Leave no litter
Safeguard water supplies
Protect wildlife, wild plants and trees
Go carefully along country roads
Respect the life of the countryside

Published 1990

Phototypesetting, printing by Higham Press Ltd., Shirland, Derbyshire

ISBN 0 907758 33 9

OLD ROAD NEAR BLACKPOOL BRIDGE. Route 3.

1

Preface

What a county of contrasts is Gloucestershire! Coming to live in the north Cotswolds 25 years ago from Derbyshire - itself a county with an exceptional scenic range - I assumed that my new locality **was** *Gloucestershire.*

How wrong can one be! Since then I have learned to appreciate that the subtle mixture that goes into the making of this unique county - the poet's 'Forest, Vale and wide blue hills' - is a walker's paradise. For whether we set off into the depths of the half-hidden Forest of Dean, stride out along the Severn's vast tidal estuary, or make for the enchanting hills and secret combes of the south Cotswolds, we are sure of discovering a world brimming with interest and beauty.

All this awaits the family prepared to use their feet. If this little book serves to encourage this to happen, it will have fulfilled its purpose.

~~~~~~~~

Acknowledgements

I should like to thank Margaret, my wife, for once more helping with the typing of my manuscript and for giving me support and encouragement.

Thank you too, to those fellow walkers who prompted me to set about the task of writing this book.

~~~~~~~~

About the author

Gordon Ottewell was formerly a headteacher in Oxfordshire and Gloucestershire. He lectures on rural affairs and writes the 'In the Country' and 'Rural Rides' features in the 'Gloucestershire Echo'.

His books on Gloucestershire include:

Wildlife Walks in the North Cotswolds (Thornhill Press).
A Cotswold Quiz Book (Barn Owl Books).
Gloucestershire - a County Quiz Book (Barn Owl Books).
Family Walks in the Cotswolds (Scarthin Books).
Theme Walks in Gloucestershire (Thornhill Press).
A Cotswold Country Diary (Barn Owl Books).

~~~~~~~~

Dedicated to a very dear friend, Winifred Spooner.

CONTENTS

MAP OF THE AREA

Numbers (5 etc.) indicate start of walk

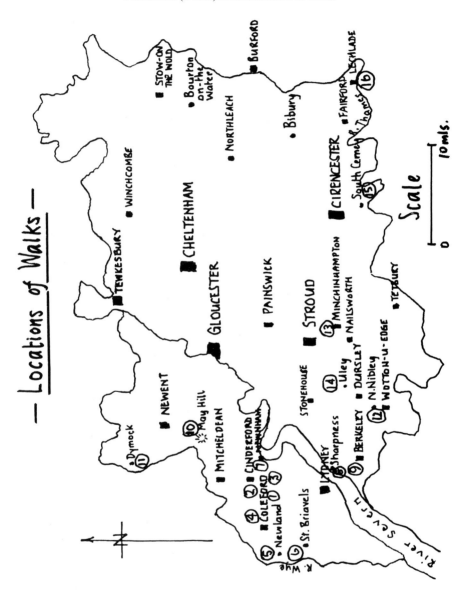

4

Introduction

The purpose of this book is to assist families with young children to explore south Gloucestershire on foot.

In an earlier volume in the 'Family Walks' series, I covered the Cotswold region from the north of the county as far south as Stroud and Cirencester. My plan here is to offer walks in the south Cotswolds, the Forest of Dean and the Severn Vale, as well as two locations in the often-overlooked north west of the county, near Newent.

As before, the walks vary in length and difficulty. Wherever possible, they are grouped according to area, although some overlapping is unavoidable. First and foremost, the aim is to encourage children to enjoy the open air, consequently the routes are planned with their interests and stamina at heart. Often, there is a pub or teashop roughly midway along the route and in most cases the more strenuous sections of the walk are tackled near the start. Road walking and retracing of steps are kept to the absolute minimum.

Under the heading 'Attractions', mention is made of some of the features along the route that are likely to appeal to children. Boredom-induced tiredness seldom arises if youngsters are interested and actively involved, and brief notes on the history and wildlife of the area, as well as unusual objects to watch out for, are included in this section.

Choosing a walk

Unless the children taking part are experienced walkers, it is advisable to choose fairly easy walks first. The appendix at the end of the book contains a list of the walks graded in order of difficulty and reference to this will help to avoid the mistake of making excessive demands on children's keenness and stamina. In any case, children will relish the anticipation of tackling more strenuous walks later. With very young children, it may be best to walk part of the route to begin with, or to arrange for the party to be picked up at some point on the route.

Allowing sufficient time

Each walk is intended as the best part of a day's outing, allowing time for play, exploring, and rest stops. It is better to over-estimate rather than under-estimate the time required; there is nothing worse than having to route-march the last stages of the walk. As a rough guide, allow a pace of around a mile per hour for very young children, graduating to two miles per hour for the experienced ten-year-old.

What to wear

The notorious British climate being what it is, it is advisable to go walking prepared for the worst! Sturdy, comfortable shoes or walking boots are preferable to wellingtons, which tire and chafe on long walks. Waterproof outer-garments, such as cagoules, are essential, while underneath, several layers of thin jumpers are better than one thick garment, as they allow more flexibility when weather conditions change. Headgear - caps and bobble hats - should not be overlooked. And don't forget a roomy rucksack in which to carry food and drink, spare clothes, maps, guides, and so on.

Finding the way

Most of the walking will be along well-marked public footpaths and bridleways and route-finding should present few difficulties. Even so, it is a good idea to take along the relevant Ordnance Survey map and sheet numbers are provided with the route directions. Occasionally, especially after a summer's growth, some stiles along public footpaths become overgrown and a walking stick can come in handy to clear the way. Sometimes too, ploughing, or some other farming activity may cause the path to be obscured. Should this occur, take the shortest possible detour round the edge of the field to regain the path.

Refreshments

Most of the pubs along the route allow children accompanied by adults into their premises. Some also have beer gardens or play areas, while others are situated near a village green or similar open space. If packed lunches are carried, remember that most landlords do not approve of such food being consumed on their premises. Closing-times should be borne in mind, especially on Sundays. Aim to arrive before 2.00 p.m. on weekdays and 1.00 p.m. on Sundays, if you are buying lunch, as catering often ceases well before closing time. Teashops usually remain open until five or six o'clock during the summer months.

Public transport

Although it is assumed that most families will travel by car, the starts of some of the walks can be reached by bus. Where available, brief details of local bus services are given after the walk descriptions and addresses of bus operators are included in the appendix.

OLD RAILWAY BRIDGE, NEW FANCY WALK

Symbols used on the route maps

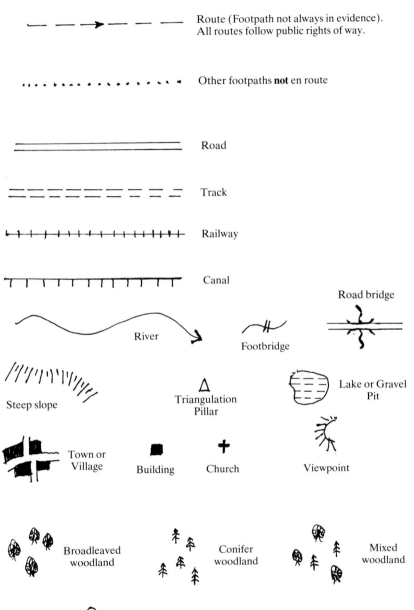

Route (Footpath not always in evidence).
All routes follow public rights of way.

Other footpaths **not** en route

Road

Track

Railway

Canal

River

Footbridge

Road bridge

Steep slope

Triangulation
Pillar

Lake or Gravel
Pit

Town or
Village

Building

Church

Viewpoint

Broadleaved
woodland

Conifer
woodland

Mixed
woodland

Number corresponds with route description

8

New Fancy Forest Walk

Outline   Car park ~ Lime avenue ~ Mineral loop line ~ Central railway ~ Forest rides ~ Railway bridge ~ Former railway line ~ Gravitation shunting sidings ~ Car park.

Summary   This short easy walk is based on the Heritage Guide published jointly by the Dean Heritage Museum and the Forestry Commission. It serves as an ideal introduction to the Forest of Dean by providing an insight into both the history and wild life of the region. Walking is along forestry roads, footpaths and old railway tracks. Apart from a climb up and descent down steps alongside the railway bridge and a gentle upward gradient towards the end of the walk, the terrain is flat throughout.

Attractions   This walk takes its name from a colliery, which operated here for over a hundred years prior to its closure in 1944. During that time it produced over 3.5 million tons of coal, which was carried away by trains of railway trucks for burning in factories and on the fires of houses many miles distant.

Part of the mining process involved removing vast quantities of rock and this was tipped alongside the mine on what was called a spoil heap. After the mine closed, much of this huge heap was removed for use in the foundations of a Welsh steelworks. The remainder was then landscaped and planted with grass and trees to create the picnic site and viewpoint we see today.

Although the New Fancy - like all the other Forest collieries - has long since disappeared, plenty of evidence can be discovered on the walk of the railways that carried the coal from the pithead on its journey to distant houses and factories. The walk starts along a cutting dug to carry a tramway. It then follows a forest road as far as the old mineral loop line along which coal trains from several local collieries were hauled by steam locomotives.

Later, the route follows the course of another railway - the so-called Forest of Dean Central - which was abandoned before it was ever put to use. On reaching the railway bridge, it is worth searching for the bench mark cut in the stonework. This marks a point 472 feet above sea level.

Perhaps the most interesting industrial relic on the walk is the stone structure passed on the last stage. This was once one of the busiest corners of the surface layout of the New Fancy Colliery. Here, loaded coal

continued on page 12

9

Route 1

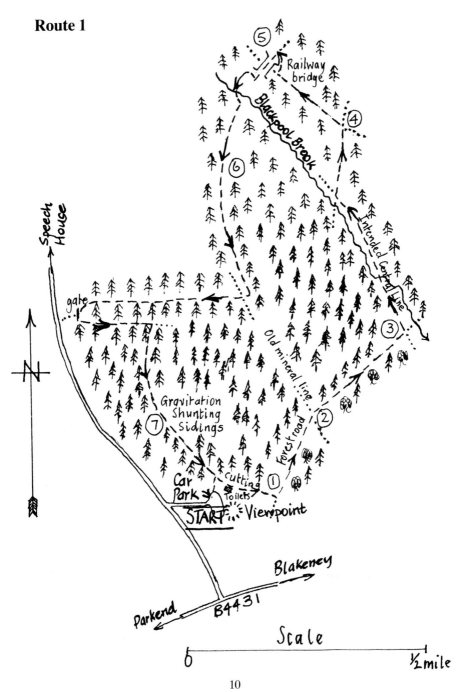

Route 1   3 miles
New Fancy Forest Walk

START   *New Fancy Car Park. New Fancy lies 1¼ miles south of the Speech House Hotel, which stands on the B4226 between Cinderford and Coleford. Alternatively, it can be reached from the B4431 (Blakeney - Parkend road). O.S. Sheet Outdoor Leisure 14 (Wye Valley & Forest of Dean) or Landranger 162 (Gloucester & Forest of Dean). G.R. 628096.*

ROUTE

To avoid confusion, the route numbers on this walk correspond with those marked in white on posts along the route.

Take the path signposted 'Forest Trail and Toilets'. At the bottom of the slope, follow red arrows on a yellow background to the right. Cross a stile to reach a T-junction.

1. *Turn left along a forest road.*
2. *At a fork, bear right.*
3. *On reaching another T-junction, turn left and soon veer right. Cross a stream to reach a junction of paths.*
4. *Ignore the red arrow indicating straight on. Instead, turn left along a grassy track to reach a railway bridge. Climb the steps to the right on to the bridge.*
5. *From the bridge, descend another flight of steps in 100 metres and cross a stream to ascend more steps and continue along the bed of an old railway.*
6. *This is a continuation of the line crossed earlier. On reaching a right turn, follow the red arrow along it. Cross a forest track and climb steadily to reach a gate at a road. Turn left before the gate along a woodland track. Where a red arrow points to the right, follow it and then keep left along a narrow undulating path. Turn left to rejoin the railway, then cross a stile near a tall stone remnant of the former colliery gravitation shunting sidings. The toilet block passed at the commencement of the walk soon appears ahead. Bear right to return to the car park.*

ACCESS BY BUS

Gloucester to Cinderford: (Red & White buses) Service 31.
Cinderford to Speech House: K. W. Beard, Cinderford.

wagons ran under their own weight down a gently sloping line and were then coupled together to form trains by men using long-handled hooks. Keen eyes are sure to spot lumps of coal and rock lying among the bushes nearby.

The greatest energy-consuming challenge remains at the end of the walk. This is the climb to the viewpoint on the summit of the old spoil heap - a must for children for the sense of achievement it provides and for parents for the fine eastward views over the treetops towards the Severn Estuary.

Refreshments   Speech House Hotel. (1¼ miles north). Morning coffee. Lunches. Garden. Children welcome.

DEER — SOPHIE RYDER

12

Forest Sculpture Trail

Outline   Car park ~ Melissa's Swing ~ Place ~ Rose in Hand ~ Black Dome ~ Fire and Water Boats ~ The Iron Road ~ Cone and Vessel ~ Deer ~ House ~ Observatory ~ The Four Seasons ~ Wind Chime ~ Cathedral ~ Car park.

Summary   Children who become bored with run-of-the-mill nature trails are in for a pleasant surprise on this walk. For instead of being expected to search for elusive flowers and listen for unco-operative birds, they get the chance to discover a collection of sculptures in different materials arranged in a woodland setting.

Parents too, are sure to find this sculpture trail stimulating, both as a pleasant walk and as a topic for discussion. How far do the sculptors - almost twenty were involved, from abroad as well as locals - succeed in interpreting the history and traditions of the Forest of Dean? Or, quite simply, is there a place for the artist in a 'natural' setting such as this? The homeward journey will certainly be enlivened by keen debate after this walk!

Attractions   A leisurely woodland ramble is a pleasant experience in its own right. In this case however, the trees play only a supportive role, for the object of the exercise is to locate - and contemplate - a series of sculptures scattered along the route.

Created from a range of materials - stone, wood, iron, wire, glass -the sculptures vary also in size and in their relationship with their natural surroundings. Some - such as Sophie Ryder's herd of deer fashioned from wire - blend in amazingly well with their woodland setting. Others, such as 'Place', a huge throne-like structure created by Magdelena Jetelova, stand out boldly in the manner of prehistoric stone circles.

The abstract nature of some of the sculptures invite speculation. 'House', by Miles Davies - a 15 foot-high rusted steel tower - could well be likened to a colliery headstocks of the kind that was scattered around the forest during its industrial prime, while it comes as no surprise to learn that the creator of 'Rose in Hand', Tim Lees, studied geology and stone masonry before embarking on his provocative stone sculpture.

In contrast, two stone carvings by Peter Randall-Page - 'Cone' and 'Vessel' - are instantly recognisable as giant representations of a pine cone and an acorn cup. Realism is strikingly conveyed too, by Keir Smith. Using 20 railway sleepers, his 'Iron Road' carvings are a fine evocation of

continued on page 16

Route 2

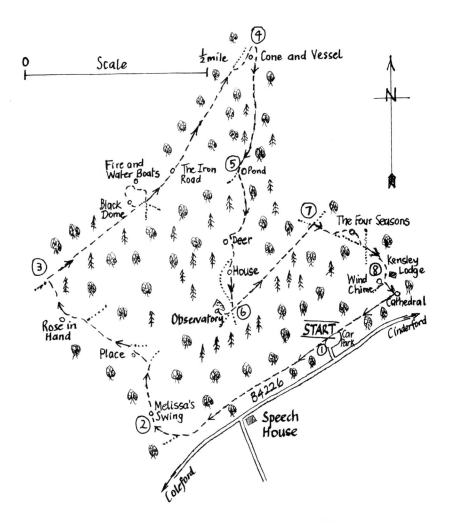

Route 2   4 miles

Forest Sculpture Trail

START *Speech House Woodland Car Park and Picnic Site, off the B4226, between Cinderford and Coleford. O.S. Sheet Outdoor Leisure 14 (Wye Valley & Forest of Dean) or Landranger 162 (Gloucester & Forest of Dean). G.R. 623124.*

ROUTE

1. *From the cattle grid, with the toilet block on the right, follow a downhill track to the left, as indicated by a yellow arrow on a tree. Ignore a right turn. When the track veers to the right, keep on along the left hand of two tracks, marked with a yellow arrow, to cross a stile. Keep straight on, with Speech House visible on the left. On reaching the Sanzen-Baker Oak, notice a blue-topped post, marked with an arrow. These posts serve as guides for the remainder of the walk. At the second post, down a slope, instead of descending to a car park, turn right to reach the first sculpture, Melissa's Swing.*

2. *From the Swing, it is only a short distance to the next feature, the vast chair-like Place. From here, the route descends to reach the Rose in Hand sculpture on the left. Beyond, continue the descent and cross a stile to reach the bed of an old railway.*

3. *Turn right along the old track. Soon, Black Dome appears on the left, and beyond can be seen Fire and Water Boats. Back on the old railway once more, cross a stile to reach Iron Road. Continue along the old line for some distance before crossing another stile on the right to follow a different old railway track, this time with original sleepers still in position. Cone and Vessel can be seen on the right.*

4. *The route now turns sharply to the right to follow a forest track as far as a pond on the left.*

5. *Here the route turns left and soon crosses a main track. At a fork, keep right. Deer soon come into view under the trees on the right (a short diversion is needed to approach them). The route continues by climbing to reach House, beyond which stands Observatory, commanding a view of a pond in which more sculptured deer can be seen. (Note: care is needed crossing the pond outflow).*

6. *Go round the pond and turn left along the main track as far as a crossroads of paths.*

B   15

7. *Turn right here and climb. In 100 metres, make a detour to the left into the trees to see The Four Seasons. Return to the main track and turn left. Cross a stile alongside a gate and climb to Wind Chime, by Kemsley Lodge.*

8. *Enter woodland to see Cathedral. From here, a straight path leads back to the car park and start.*

ACCESS BY BUS
Gloucester to Cinderford: (Red & White buses). Service 31.
Cinderford to Speech House: K. W. Beard, Cinderford.

---

such commonplace features as a feather, a leaf and a forest stream, as well as industrial themes.

The likelihood is that Peter Appleton's work will win him pride of place as far as children are concerned. 'Melissa's Swing' provides both musical and practical fun, while 'Wind Chime' is sure to please as tired walkers near the end of the 4-mile route.

Extra interest is provided along the route in searching for the remains of other sculptures, made from less durable materials, traces of which can still be spotted by observant young eyes.

Refreshments Speech House Hotel. Morning coffee. Lunches. Garden. Children welcome.

TYNDALE
MONUMENT

16

Soudley and Mallards Pike

Outline Soudley village ~ Staple Edge ~ Mallards Pike Lake ~ Blackpool Bridge ~ Drummer Boy Stone ~ Soudley village.

Summary This walk is intended to provide a taste of the real Forest of Dean. It is a woodland walk from beginning to end, and apart from the areas around Mallards Pike Lake and Blackpool Bridge, is routed along forest roads and footpaths well away from popular centres. Combined with a visit to the Dean Heritage Centre, close to the starting point, the walk enables visitors of all ages to appreciate the part played by forestry and industry in shaping the forest we know today. The actual walking should present no difficulties to families accustomed to country rambling. Careful reading of the route instructions is advisable however, for landmarks of the kind taken for granted in open country are conspicuous by their absence in the heart of the forest!

Attractions It would be a very insensitive person indeed who did not feel a thrill of anticipation on leaving behind the bustle of the workaday world to plunge into the heart of the forest. That is exactly what happens on this walk and children in particular, will sense the enchantment as the leaf canopy closes overhead. For the light takes on a greenish shade of its own and the towering trees crowd in on every side as the tempo of life itself adjusts to the changeless unhurried pace of the living forest.

Whatever the season, the forest possesses its own brand of magic. In spring, the pale purple haze of bluebells is almost breathtaking in its perfection. In high summer, the sleepy drone of insects and the shafts of sunlight piercing the leaves create an equally distinctive atmosphere. While the changing colours and drifting leaves of autumn and winter bestow their own sad beauty on the woodland scene.

Birds - tits, treecreepers, woodpeckers and warblers - are ceaselessly active high above, while dragonflies abound in the sunny clearings of summer. There is always the chance of glimpsing deer along the lonely rides and shade-loving butterflies gladden summer walks.

History, too, is never far away. The Drummer Boy Stone is thought to have been a primitive iron-smelting bowl while the cobbled section of road near Blackpool Bridge, although not now considered to be Roman, is certainly centuries old.

The deep coal pits of the Dean may have gone but the drift workings of the so-called freeminers can still be seen along the route. These men

continued on page 20

Route 3

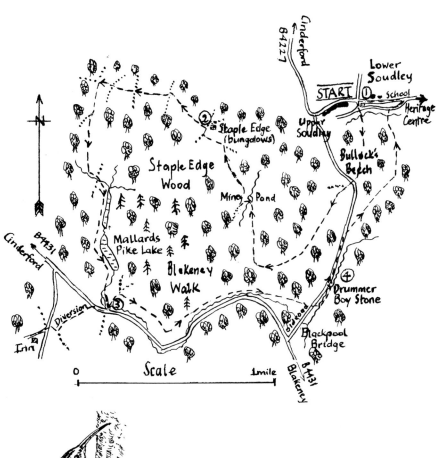

TREECREEPER. Brown and White. 13cm.

18

Route 3   6½ miles
Soudley and Mallards Pike

START   *Soudley village, on B4227, between Cinderford and Blakeney. Park just off the road on the Heritage Centre side of the primary school. O.S. Sheet Outdoor Leisure 14 (Wye Valley & Forest of Dean) or Landranger 162 (Gloucester & Forest of Dean). G.R. 661105.*

ROUTE

1. *Walk along the pavement towards the White Horse Inn. Turn left down Lower Road, keeping straight on at a right hand bend to cross one of two bridges. Bear right to cross a stile alongside a gate into woodland. (Yellow arrows indicate the way as far as Mallards Pike Lake). Keep left at a fork and climb to cross a road. At a barrier, turn right and keep along the main track, which soon veers to the left, ignoring other possibilities. Cross a stile alongside a gate. The path now climbs to the right, offering splendid views. Beyond a cattle grid, ignore two tracks to the right. Soon, the track swings right and then left to pass a small pond on the right. In 50 metres, turn sharp right up a narrow track (before reaching a mine visible ahead). More signs of mining are passed on the left before a crossroads of tracks is reached. Cross over and take a right fork under conifers to reach a main track. Turn left here to reach Staple Edge Lodge (two bungalows). Follow the garden hedge round to the right as far as the gate of the first bungalow.*

2. *Directly opposite, take a descending grassy path under the trees. Cross over two tracks, then a stream, and a third track to reach a fourth cross-track at the top of a slope. Turn left, and in 200 metres, left again along a narrow woodland path. This path eventually follows a stream on the right to reach Mallards Pike Lake. Keep along the right bank before eventually leaving the yellow-arrow route to pass the Lancaster footbridge and reach a barrier and a metalled road. Turn left over a bridge and keep straight on towards the B4431.*

    Diversion to Rising Sun Inn: Go over a cattle grid and turn right along the B4431. In 100 metres, directly opposite the Forestry Commission notice indicating Mallards Pike Lake, strike off left over open ground, heading between overgrown spoil heaps and a conifer plantation. The faint path leads to the right of the plantation to a barrier. Turn right here to reach a road. The Rising Sun Inn is reached along the drive opposite.

3. *To continue the walk from the approach to the cattle grid near the B4431, turn sharp left through the barrier and climb to a fork in the track. Take the right fork. Pass an old mine on the left and follow the*

19

track all the way down to a road. The remnant of old road at Blackpool Bridge can be inspected some distance beyond the stream on the right. The route crosses the road ahead and turns left along a narrow woodland path parallel to the road. In 200 metres, cross a footbridge on the left to see the Drummer Boy Stone by the roadside.

4. *Turn right along the road and, 50 metres after passing a parking sign opposite a metalled track on the right, take a curving track climbing on the right. Cross a metalled track and continue into woods along a narrow path. On reaching the gardens of some houses, turn left to reach a metalled track. Keep on along it, passing a cross-track before dipping to the left of Rock House along the line of a power line. Soudley school can now be seen ahead. Pass the Comrades Club and follow the road over a stream and up to the starting point.*

ACCESS BY BUS
Soudley Valley buses connect Soudley with Cinderford and Lydney.

---

after serving an apprenticeship of a year and a day, had to register with an official called the Gaveller - a mining custom established as long ago as the 13th century in the Forest of Dean.

There is insufficient space to consider forestry here. That omission will be rectified on the next walk.

Refreshments The Rising Sun Inn, Moseley Green. Bar meals. Children welcome. Old mine wheel and mining relics on view.

PIED FLYCATCHER.

Black and White. 13cm.

Route 4

Cannop, Nagshead and Parkend

Outline Cannop Ponds car park, Folder's Green ~ Nagshead Plantation ~ Parkend ~ Cannop Ponds ~ Car park.

Summary This is a forest walk with trees and woodland birds as the main interests but with the industrial history of the Parkend area thrown in for good measure. Apart from the Parkend section, the walk is along forest roads and paths throughout and is nowhere difficult. As with all forest walks, however, care should be taken to follow the route methodically, for landmarks are few and far between.

Attractions Few visitors lingering along the dappled margins of Cannop Ponds realise that they owe their enjoyment to 19th century industrial endeavour. For the two ponds were created by the damming of the Cannop Brook to provide water power for the iron works which once dominated the scene around Parkend. Now an attraction for anglers, birdwatchers and walkers, the ponds are stocked with fish and are rich in plant and animal life. Coots, moorhens and mallard dabble in the open water, while the shallows prove an irresistible lure to children.

Industry has not altogether disappeared from the region. The last surviving stone works passed along the route is still busy with the cutting and loading of the Pennant sandstone quarried nearby, which is in great demand for use in ornamental masonry.

Once into the Nagshead Plantation however, the real forest atmosphere takes over. Many of the giant deciduous trees, especially the oaks, date from pre-Victorian times. Their planting was carried out under the direction of Edward Machen, deputy surveyor of the forest, who was responsible for the re-stocking of 11,000 acres of neglected woodland. Oak was of great importance for shipbuilding in the days before iron warships. Machen also planted a mixture of Spanish (sweet) chestnut, beech and sycamore, as well as conifers - fir, pine and larch - which have been extensively grown in recent years by the Forestry Commission.

The R.S.P.B.'s Nagshead reserve contains fine old oakwoods ideal for birds. Children will enjoy spotting the nestboxes along the route. Over 300 of these were occupied in 1988, chiefly by blue and great tits and pied flycatchers - handsome black and white birds for which the Nagshead reserve is especially noted.

The village of Parkend is quiet now, compared with a century or so ago. Then, coal mines, iron and tin works, lime kilns and tramroads made

continued on page 24

21

Route 4

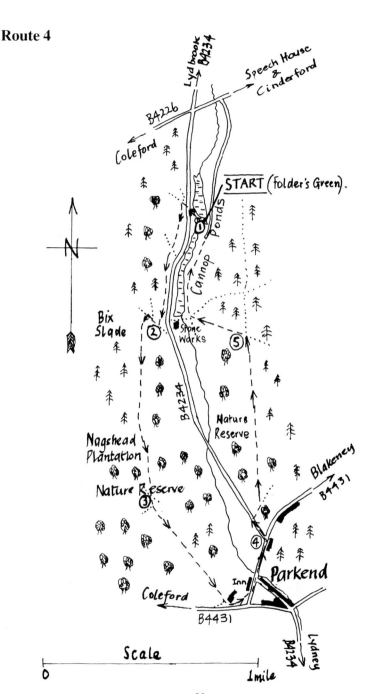

Route 4   4½ miles
Cannop, Nagshead and Parkend

START   *Cannop Ponds car park, Folder's Green, reached from the B4226, ½ mile south west from the Speech House Hotel, and approached along a forest road. O.S. Sheet Outdoor Leisure 14 (Wye Valley & Forest of Dean) or Landranger 162 (Gloucester & Forest of Dean). G.R. 610107.*

ROUTE

1. *From the Forestry Commission stone information pillar, cross the footbridge along the path indicated as a forest trail. Keep a pond on the right as far as the B4234. Cross carefully and follow a forest track. In 80 metres, fork left at a marker post, following a yellow arrow into coniferous woodland. In 150 metres, turn left as indicated by a green arrow. Cross a green ride into more woodland, this time of a mixed variety.*

2. *Opposite the stone works, follow the green arrow to the right to reach a forest road near its junction with the B4234. Turn right along it and keep straight on, ignoring a track climbing to the right. In a short distance, turn left by a power pole and climb to cross a stile into Nagshead Plantation. The R.S.P.B. Reserve is on the right. Keep straight on, crossing 2 more stiles to reach the R.S.P.B. car park.*

3. *Follow the forest road as far as a grassy path on the left, just before a sharp bend to the right. Follow this path by a factory fence alongside the road into Parkend. (The Woodman Inn is on the left). The walk continues along the B4431 as far as its junction with the B4234 (Lydney road).*

4. *Turn left here and then right along a forest road marked Cannop Valley Nature Reserve. At a junction, bear left round a barrier and keep straight on as far as a crossroads of tracks with a stile straight ahead.*

5. *Turn left here, following a green arrow. Just before a stile marked with a yellow arrow, turn left and drop down a bank. Cross the old railway bed slightly to the left to a post marked with green and yellow arrows. Just beyond, instead of crossing the footbridge, follow the arrows along the bank of the pond (signposted Christchurch 3¾ miles) back through the trees to the start.*

ACCESS BY BUS
Gloucester to Cinderford: Red & White buses. Service 31.
Cinderford to Speech House: K. W. Beard, Cinderford.

it the chief industrial centre of the Forest. Now however, all that remain of that bustling past are traces of the railway and the tall distinctive building that was once the blowing engine house for the ironworks, and which now serves as a field study centre.

Leaving Parkend to its memories, the route plunges once more into woodland, with another opportunity for bird watching and flower and insect spotting on the way back to the waterside car park.

Refreshments   Woodman Inn, Parkend. Bar meals.
Tearoom, Parkend. Cooked meals and cream teas.

THE BUCKSTONE

Newland and Staunton stones

Outline   Newland ~ High Meadow Farm ~ Staunton ~ Toad's Mouth ~ Buckstone ~ Knockalls Lodge ~ Furnace Grove ~ Newland.

Summary   This walk, and the one that follows, explores the western extremities of the Forest of Dean - a fascinating corner of Gloucestershire bordering the Wye valley. Perhaps the most noticeable difference is that a good deal of the walking is over open country, with woodland less evident than to the east. Nevertheless, this is an integral part of the Forest, and contains some of the most ancient and romantic of its features, as this varied and by no means difficult walk reveals.

Attractions   The walk begins at Newland, a modest little village today, but deservedly famous for two remarkable buildings. One is the old grammar school founded in the 16th century by Edward Bell. The other is All Saints' Church, often referred to as 'The Cathedral of the Forest'. A visit to this fine 13th century church is strongly recommended. It contains some striking old brasses, including one which depicts a miner with his candle in his mouth, and carrying a pickaxe and a hod.

    The other village on the route is Staunton (not to be confused with another village of the same name, situated between Gloucester and Ledbury). It, too, is well worth a leisurely exploration, for, like Newland, it contains some of the oldest buildings in the Forest.

    But it is Staunton's stones that account for much of its appeal. With one exception they are natural features, as it old name - Stane, or Stone Town - indicates. They are composed of old red sandstone and pebbles of quartz, a mixture known as quartz conglomerate, or pudding stone, fragments of which can be seen lying around throughout the Forest.

    The first stone encountered is Toad's Mouth Rock. Children will soon see how it got its name, although no doubt many will think up more fanciful names, especially when told that in prehistoric times, law-breakers were supposed to have been beheaded on the rock's flat top.

    The Buckstone, visited soon afterwards, was a delicately poised rocking stone until a group of irresponsible merrymakers toppled it from its lofty perch in 1885. It is said that, by gentle rocking, it could be used to send messages across the nearby woods, and that gamekeepers used its vibrations to trap deer poachers this way. Sadly, the Buckstone's rocking days are over. It is now fixed to its base by concrete and an iron pin.

continued on page 28

25

Route 5

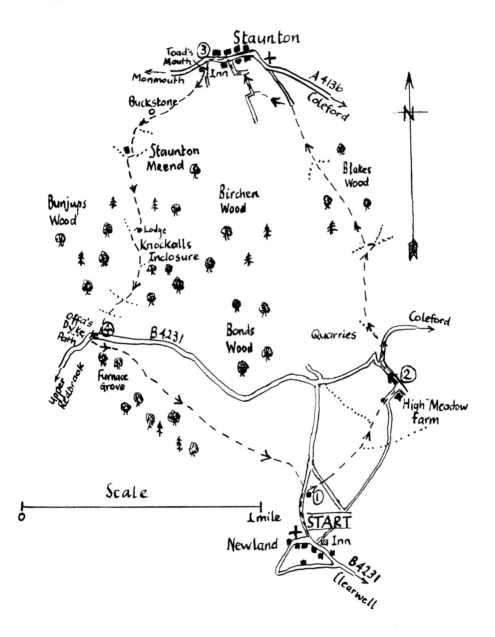

Staunton

Toad's Mouth ③

Monmouth

Inn

A 4136
Coleford

Buckstone ○

Staunton Meend

Blakes Wood

Bunjups Wood

Birchen Wood

Lodge
Knockalls Inclosure

Offa's Dyke Path

B 4231

Bonds Wood

Quarries

Coleford

Upper Redbrook

Furnace Grove

High Meadow Farm ②

Scale

0 — 1 mile

START ①
Inn

Newland

B 4231
Clearwell

N

Route 5   5½ miles
Newland and Staunton stones

START *Newland village, on the B4231 (Lydney - Monmouth road).*
O.S. Sheet Outdoor Leisure 14 (Wye Valley & Forest of Dean) or
Landranger 162 (Gloucester & Forest of Dean. G.R. 554095. Park in
village.

ROUTE

1. *Walk along the village street (B4231) in the direction of Redbrook and*
   Monmouth. On the edge of the village, where two signposts indicate
   footpaths on either side of the road, follow the right hand path by a
   house. Go through a gate, over a stile, and across a field. Go over a lane
   and cross a series of stiles to reach a fork in the path. Take the left fork,
   aiming for a white bungalow ahead. Go through the gate to the right of
   the bungalow to reach a track. Pass farm buildings (High Meadow
   Farm) on the right and climb to a road.

2. *Turn left to reach another road. Now turn right, and in a short distance -*
   at a right hand bend - turn left along a wide track. In 20 metres, turn right
   along a narrow track under the trees. On reaching a wider track, turn
   right along it, passing a quarry on the left. Ignore side turns. At a
   crossroads of tracks, turn left and in 50 metres, right along a narrow
   path between trees. After a steady climb, reach another crossroads of
   tracks. Go over and continue along a grassy ride, which soon descends
   to Staunton. Where the ride joins a lane, bear left away from the lane
   and continue to reach a metalled road. Turn right and then left at a
   Monmouth signpost before climbing to the right to reach the White Hart
   Inn at Staunton.

3. *From the inn, follow the Monmouth road for 50 metres before turning*
   left along a lane. The Toad's Mouth rock is on the right. Follow the
   yellow arrow up the bank on the right just before a gate and 15 m.p.h.
   sign. The Buckstone is reached after a steady climb (on the right by a
   triangulation pillar). From the Buckstone, descend for 50 metres to a
   signpost. Now keep straight on, along the route indicated Redbrook. At
   a metalled track, turn right and then left, passing Buckstone Lodge to
   reach a metalled drive. Newland can be seen in the distance straight
   ahead. Turn right and go as far as a gate to a house. Turn left here and
   go down a clear path, keeping a fence on the right, to a metalled track.
   Turn right here to pass Knockalls Lodge and then left at a fork beyond a
   barrier. At the next fork, go right and descend to a third fork. (Glorious

views ahead). Take the right fork and go over a crossroads of tracks and descend steeply to a wider track. Follow the yellow arrow straight across this, still descending, and cross 3 stiles to reach the B4231.

4. *Turn right (no pavement) and cross into Wales. 50 metres round a bend in the road, turn left along a signposted footpath. Cross a footbridge and climb over stiles, go through a field and into woodland. (Furnace Grove). From the wood, the path continues over stiles by field edges before becoming a clear track, which reaches Newland opposite the path taken at the start of the walk. Turn right to finish.*

Apart from the novelty provided by the stones, children successfully completing this walk will be able to boast that they left both Gloucestershire and England in the process! This comes about because after descending from Knockall's Inclosure to the B4231, the route briefly enters the Welsh county of Gwent before climbing through Furnace Grove and back over the fields to Newland.

Families driving along the A4136 from Staunton towards Coleford may care to watch out for the man-made Long Stone, a 7 foot-high survivor of the Bronze Age.

Refreshments   White Hart Inn, Staunton. Bar meals.
Ostrich Inn, Newland. Bar meals. Afternoon tea.

ST. BRIAVELS CASTLE

28

Route 6

St. Briavels and Wye Valley

Outline St. Briavels village ~ Offa's Dyke Path ~ Bigsweir Bridge ~ Lindor's Farm ~ St. Briavels.

Summary Few short walks can rival this for variety. An historic village complete with ancient castle, a section of one of the most scenic long-distance footpaths in Britain, a stretch along an equally renowned river spanned by a Telford bridge - all this, plus an abundance of wild life, combines to make a memorable visit to this south-western corner of Gloucestershire and the Forest of Dean.

   The walking, especially on the first stretch of the route, is somewhat demanding by Gloucestershire standards, but the rewards are such that despite a stiff climb towards the end, every member of the family is sure to find something to enjoy and recall with pleasure long afterwards.

Attractions The hilltop village of St. Briavels was once the administrative centre of the Royal Hunting Forest of Dean. Centuries before other, bigger towns and villages developed, its castle, perched 800 feet above the Wye valley, was the home of the king's Constable, who was also Warden of the Forest. His emblem, a hunting horn, can still be seen carved above a crown on a high chimney of the entrance gateway.

   Sadly, much of the castle has gone. The great keep collapsed in the 18th century and the moat has long been drained. Despite all this, it remains an impressive sight. Its gateway dates from 1275 and it still retains a prison on the first floor and a dungeon below. Now serving as a youth hostel, it must surely be the oldest of its kind in the country.

   An ancient custom that takes place in St. Briavels on Whit Sunday can be traced back to the 13th century. This is the 'Bread and Cheese' ceremony, at which this food is thrown to the crowd while the vicar recites: 'St. Briavels water and Whynols wheat are the best bread and water King John did ever eat'.

   One of the wells that once provided this renowned water is passed early on the walk. Notice the hart's tongue fern thriving in the damp shade. Other distinctive ferns growing along the route include the handsome male fern and common polypody. Keen young botanists should identify wood sage and wood spurge along the shady sections and hemp nettle and golden saxifrage by the hillside streams.

   Prominent along the Wyre are two introduced plants. Himalayan balsam is easily recognised by its pink flowers. Japanese knotweed grows

continued on page 32

29

Route 6

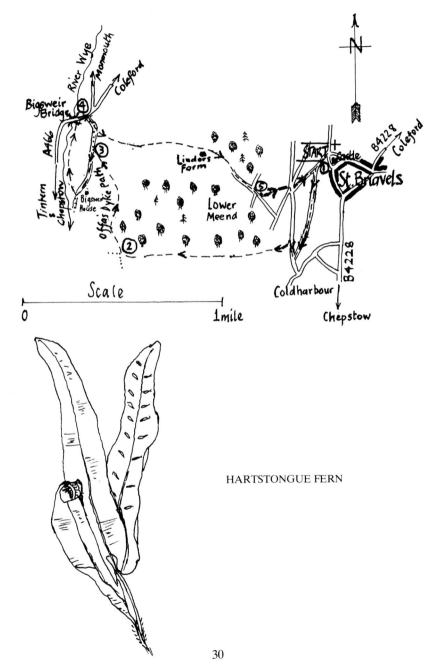

HARTSTONGUE FERN

30

Route 6   4½ miles
St. Briavels and Wye Valley

START   *St. Briavels village, just off the B4228 between Coleford and Chepstow. Park near the castle. O.S. Sheet Outdoor Leisure 14 (Wye Valley & Forest of Dean) or Landranger 162 (Gloucester & Forest of Dean). G.R. 558047.*

ROUTE

1. *Follow the signpost 'Lower Meend ½', down Cinder Hill. Soon, at a junction, fork left along Lower Road, passing an old well on the left. At a steep-angled junction, turn right and descend a road as far as a signposted footpath on the left. Follow this path for 20 metres, towards Firtree Cottage, then go down stone steps on the right and cross a footbridge over a stream. The route now enters woodland, with a stone wall on the left for some distance. Watch for yellow arrows. Beyond the wall, ignore side turns, including any marked with arrows.* **Care is needed as there is a steep drop to the right.**

2. *In about a mile, the route reaches the Offa's Dyke long-distance footpath (marked with an acorn symbol). Turn right along this path, descending steeply, down steps at first, through woodland. Leave the woodland over a stile. The route continues to descend across a large field, with Bigsweir Bridge ahead to the left. After passing through an avenue of veteran sweet chestnut trees, keep on down a field to reach the drive to Bigsweir House.*

3. *Turn left along the drive and after going through a gateway, keep on as far as a stile on the right (marked with the acorn symbol). There follows a stretch of riverside walking as far as Bigsweir Bridge.*

4. *On reaching the road at the bridge, do not cross the river. Instead, turn right and follow the road for a short distance (no pavement) to regain the drive walked along earlier. Follow this drive as far as the fork leading to Lindor's Farm. Continue, passing the farm on your right and keep straight on to cross a dilapidated stile to the left of a metal gate. Climb a field with trees on the left. 40 metres before reaching a hedge at the top, follow the yellow arrow under the trees on the left to cross a stile alongside a gate. Turn right up a lane. Ignore a left turn. Shortly after passing a phone box, turn left along a signposted path by Cherry Tree Cottage.*

5. *Keep climbing past cottages to reach a road. Turn right and, ignoring 2 minor roads on the right, climb round a bend and turn right at a fork to reach St. Briavels and the start.*

in dense thickets and has broad pointed leaves. It has become a nuisance by spreading widely and choking other plants.

Bigsweir Bridge was designed by Thomas Telford for St. Augustine's at Bristol but instead was erected at its present site in 1824. The Wye is tidal as far as the bridge and one of the most impressive sights along its bank is that of salmon leaping from the water as they battle up river to their spawning grounds.

Refreshments   George Inn, St. Briavels. Bar meals. Garden.

Crown Inn, St. Briavels. Bar meals. Garden.

Baytree restaurant.

NEWNHAM-ON-SEVERN

32

Route 7

5 miles

Newnham and Blaize Bailey

Outline   Newnham-on-Severn ∼ The Culver House ∼ Blaize Bailey Farm ∼ Blaize Bailey Viewpoint ∼ Blaize Bailey Farm ∼ Newnham.

Summary   This walk links the ancient little town of Newnham with the eastern edge of the Forest of Dean. It entails a steady climb on the outward journey but this is rewarded by the superb views obtainable from two viewpoints - one overlooking the Arlingham loop of the Severn estuary and the other taking in the forest panorama westwards towards Soudley. The route directions may appear somewhat detailed as some of the footpaths are seldom used, but with care, little difficulty should be experienced on this delightful walk.

Attractions   If the views already mentioned appeal chiefly to the adults in the party, this in no way implies that the younger members of the family will miss out on this walk. The little town of Newnham-on-Severn has plenty to interest everyone, including two rather unusual 'firsts'. The first greenhouse was built here by Sir Edward Mansell during the 17th century, using locally made glass, while many years later, in 1809, an old tramway tunnel under nearby Haie Hill was converted for use by the newly invented railway and became the first-ever railway tunnel.

Before the digging of the Sharpness - Gloucester canal, Newnham was a busy port. Trading ships came and went and the sands attracted day -trippers from the Forest of Dean. Both ships and sands have now gone, for the river Severn shifted its course, leaving Newnham still a riverside town, but without its former importance. Of its 20 inns, only three remain, one of which, the Victoria, is said to be haunted by the ghost of a chambermaid!

A mystery of a different kind awaits along the route. On the edge of the Forest, before the climb up to the Blaize Bailey Viewpoint, stand the ruins of several cottages. In fact, it appears that there was a hamlet here until a few years ago. Why were the cottages abandoned? Why has no one renovated them and moved in? What are the drawbacks to life in a lonely country cottage? Food for thought - and lively discussion - in plenty!

But if people shun living in this remote spot, the same cannot be said for wild life. For as well as the sheep that flourish on these slopes, the Forest fringe is rich in bird life. Gaudy jays squawk in the oaks, green woodpeckers laugh as they bound from tree to tree, and flocks of dainty long-tailed tits search nimbly for food in the upper boughs. Watch too, for

continued on page 36

Route 7

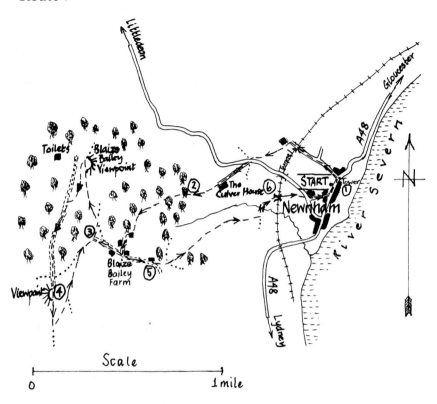

JAY.
Reddish Brown, Blue, Black and White. 34cm.

34

Route 7   5 miles
Newnham and Blaize Bailey

START   *Newnham on Severn. Park along service road parallel to the
main street (A48). O.S. Sheet Landranger 162 (Gloucester and Forest
of Dean) or Outdoor Leisure 14 (Wye Valley & Forest of Dean). G.R.
691118.*

ROUTE

1. *Walk down the main street (A48) and turn left along Station Road,
opposite the Clock Tower. The road continues as a lane. Cross a railway
bridge and, where Hyde Lane bends to the right, keep straight on for 30
metres as far as a footpath sign. Take this path and cross a stile by a
cottage. Bear half-right across a field to reach a second stile. In the next
field, the path keeps to a similar line to reach another stile at a road.
Cross carefully and, instead of following the footpath directly opposite,
take the surfaced lane to the right, which climbs with a wood on the left.
At a fork, keep right and cross a stile by farm buildings (The Culver
House). Follow the track ahead towards woodland.*

2. *Enter the wood over the right-hand of 2 stiles by a pylon and keep
straight on, climbing under the trees. Enter a field by a pylon and with
woodland now on the right, continue ascending before dipping
diagonally left towards the right hand of 2 barns. Instead of entering the
woodland by the barn, turn left along the boundary fence, following a
sunken lane as far as the second barn. Here, cross a stile by the barn wall
to follow a clear track flanked by a wall on the left and trees on the right.
At the second of 2 ruined cottages, turn right and pass a farmyard to
enter woodland along a wide track. Ignore side tracks and climb to a
T-junction (Yellow arrow).*

3. *Turn right along a forest road and climb to the walled viewpoint on the
right. (Blaize Bailey). On leaving the viewpoint, climb the steps
opposite as far as the first woodland path on the left. (Toilets and
Forestry Commission map straight ahead). Follow the path and swing
right along it to pass a brick water tank and reach the main forest road.
Turn left along this and ignore side turns to reach another viewpoint on
the right overlooking Soudley.*

4. *Continuing, take the first track on the left. This bends back sharply.
Ignore a sharp right turn and keep on to rejoin the outward route at the
T-junction marked with the yellow arrow (3). Turn right and retrace
steps as far as the ruined cottage. Here, leave the outward route by*

keeping straight on through a gate and along a grassy track, which eventually veers right by a barn.

5. *Turn left here to follow the line of the barn wall down a field to a stile. Keep on down a raised bank, following woodland round to a stile on the left. Bear half-right across a sloping field, aiming in the direction of a distant white house visible between a large ash tree and woodland. Cross a stile by the woodland edge and, keeping a fence on the left, descend a large field. Cross a stile into another field and then another leading across the bottom of an orchard. Go through a gap in the trees ahead and immediately turn right over a stile and a bridge. Head for the power pole straight ahead and cross the railway bridge.*

6. *Cross a stile and climb a field to a gravelled path which leads to a road via a stile. Cross the road and turn right along the raised pavement into Newnham.*

---

grey squirrels scurrying for cover at your approach. The downhill return walk to Newnham is over quiet fields with enticing glimpses of the mighty Severn ahead. Any remaining energy can be consumed climbing up to the church, from which excellent southward views can be had of the river that brought fame to Newnham -and then took it away again.

Refreshments   There are inns, as already stated, in Newnham but none on the route. Why not take a picnic and eat it at the Blaize Bailey Viewpoint?

HULK OF SEVERN TROW

Route 8

Option 1 - Canal Walk only - 4½ miles
Option 2 - Circular walk - 4¾ miles

Sharpness Canal

Outline   **Option 1:** Sharpness ~ Canal towpath ~ Purton (and return).
Option 2: Sharpness ~ Canal towpath ~ Purton ~ Hinton ~ Canal bridge ~ Sharpness.

Summary   This is the only walk in the book in which families are encouraged to retrace their steps, rather than embark on a circular walk. Directions for a circular route are given for those to whom retracing, no matter how pleasurable the walk, is to be avoided at all costs, but an unremarkable inland walk over little-used paths seems something of an anti-climax after an absorbing beginning.

That beginning is a 2¼-mile walk along the Gloucester and Sharpness Canal, from Sharpness Docks to Purton. Flat and straightforward it may be but the varied sights along the route are sure to appeal to every member of the family.

Attractions   The walk starts at Sharpness Docks, built, together with the Gloucester and Sharpness Canal, to promote the city of Gloucester as a trading port. Until the opening of the canal, in 1827, ships faced a difficult 30-mile journey along the Severn to reach the city. The canal almost halved that distance, and was dug to allow for vessels of up to 1,000 tons to navigate its entire length. Today, the Gloucester and Sharpness is the only working canal in the county and lighters and barges carry timber, grain and petroleum products which have been transferred from larger sea-going vessels at Sharpness Docks.

But it is the rotting hulks of old vessels, rather than the occasional modern lighter or barge, that stir the imagination on this walk. Known as trows, these sailing boats were the equivalent of today's heavy goods vehicles in bygone times, carrying their cargoes to and fro along the river highway. Their work done, they were unceremoniously beached along the shore and lie now like skeletons, picked clean by the weather.

Another ruin sure to arouse interest along the route is the tower-like abutment of the old Severn railway bridge, demolished in 1969 after being badly damaged by colliding barges.

The canal-side walk is ideal for bird watching. Depending on the state of the tide, there is usually plenty of activity on the estuary mud or by the water. Large flocks of gulls - chiefly of the black-headed or lesser black-backed varieties - forage for food, together with large handsome

continued on page 40

37

Route 8

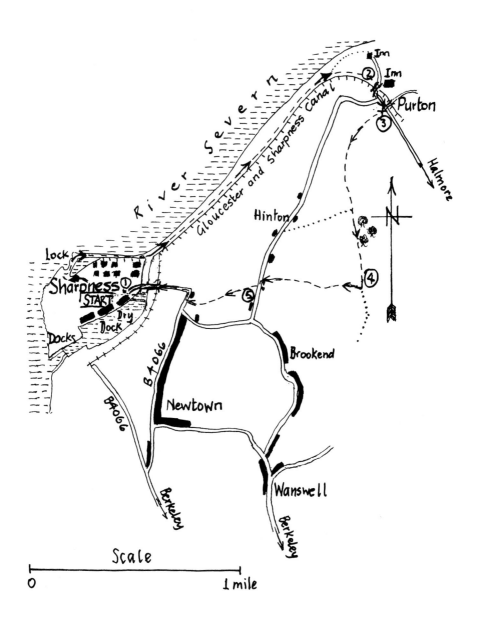

Scale

0   1 mile

Route 8

Option 1: Canal walk only - 4½ miles
Option 2: Circular walk - 4¾ miles

Sharpness Canal

START   *Sharpness. Approach along the B4066 via Wanswell. At a T-junction, bear right. The road swings sharp left and crosses the canal. Park on the waste ground on the right. O.S. Sheets Landranger 162 (Gloucester & Forest of Dean) or Outdoor Leisure 14 (Wye Valley & Forest of Dean). G.R. 672028.*

ROUTE

1. *Take the Severn Way Path on the right. Pass the Sharpness Centre, also on the right, and follow the metalled path down to the estuary. Cross a lock by the bridge and pass a house on the left. Continue along the towpath, eventually passing the hulks of old Severn trows on the left. In 2¼ miles lies Purton (Berkeley Hunt Inn).*

2. *From Purton,* **either** *retrace your steps to Sharpness* **or** *continue on the circular walk by crossing the bridge and turning left along the road signposted Halmore and Berkeley to reach the church.*

3. *Alongside the church, take the signposted footpath. Go through a handgate and over the corner of a field to a field gate on the right of a cottage. Follow the yellow arrow up the field ahead in the direction of a power line. (If growing crops make this difficult, the climb can be made along the right-hand edge of the field). Leave the field at the top left hand corner through a gate. Keep a hedge on the right through 2 handgates. The hedge is now on the left. Enter a large field through another handgate and keep straight on to meet a grassy track with a hedge still on the left. When the track swings to the right, keep straight on, following the hedge on the left under power lines to another handgate where the field tapers to an end.*

4. *Instead of passing through the gate, turn right and follow the hedge down the field. Just before the bottom left-hand corner, go through a gap, keeping the hedge on the right. After passing through another gate, cross a stream and pass a power line post to reach a gateway beyond. Follow the hedge on the right up the field to reach a road through a gate by a bungalow. Turn left and in 60 metres, turn right through a metal gate opposite Malt House Cottage. (This section of the walk was not signposted at the time the route was planned and the going was difficult. Those wishing to avoid this section should pass the metal gate, then turn right and right again to reach the canal bridge and the start).*

39

5. *From the gate, the route passes through an old orchard, with a hedge on the right. Leave through a gate into a field. Head for the lefthand corner. Cranes at Sharpness can be seen ahead. In the next field, keep a hedge on the right and descend to a stile and a road. Turn right along it and then left over the canal bridge and back to the start.*

ACCESS BY BUS

Circle Line Coaches - services linking Sharpness with Gloucester, Dursley and Stroud.

---

shelduck and several species of waders. Occasionally, a heron can be seen standing motionless in the shallows and large black cormorants fly low and straight over the water.

Those families completing the circular walk will experience a contrasting inland scene as they follow undulating footpaths over quiet if unspectacular countryside before coming in sight of the dockland panorama of Sharpness once more, where any time remaining can be well spent watching life in this busy little dock.

Refreshments   The Berkeley Hunt Inn, Purton. Bar snacks. Garden.

JENNER MUSEUM, BERKELEY

Route 9

Round and about Berkeley

Outline Berkeley ~ Berkeley Pill ~ Severn Way Path ~ Oakhunger Farm ~ Hook Street ~ Berkeley.

Summary Like the previous walk, this route offers easy pleasant walking along a stretch of the Severn estuary. The actual Severn-side section is short, for the walk begins in the little town of Berkeley and then follows a stream (the Berkeley Pill) for some distance. The last stage of the route is inland and along little-used footpaths and bridleways. If an early start is made there will be plenty of time left in which to see the town itself and visit the unusual church, the Jenner museum and the famous castle standing in its deer park.

Attractions Few small towns can boast such a spread of historical associations as Berkeley, set close by the Severn estuary in south Gloucestershire. Two vast buildings - one old, one new -dominate the scene for miles around. Although not on the actual route, most families will wish to devote part of the time to a tour of the fine 12th century castle, the home of the Berkeley family and the place at which King Edward II was murdered in 1322. As well as the castle tour, the price of admission includes a visit to the butterfly house, 30 acres of magnificent gardens and a walk through the park containing red and fallow deer.

There can be no greater contrast between this ancient castle and Berkeley nuclear power station, which was built by the Severn west of the town in the 1950s and was de-commissioned in 1989. This was one of the earliest British nuclear power stations and although now obsolete and no longer producing power, its distinctive outline will remain a feature of the estuary for many years to come.

The short stretch of estuary walking is full of interest for the young naturalist. Gulls, cormorants, oystercatchers and herons feed along the shoreline and flocks of lapwings often congregate on the low-lying fields inland. The beach also provides suitable habitat for common saltwater-loving plants. It was this beach and these fields that were the happy hunting ground for the young Edward Jenner, Berkeley's most illustrious son. The boy who studied hedgehogs, cuckoos and dolphins here went on to become the world-famous doctor whose life was dedicated to eradicating the deadly smallpox. The story of how he vaccinated a local boy, James Phipps, with cowpox from an infected milkmaid, makes fascinating reading and a visit to the Jenner museum, including the little

continued on page 44

Route 9

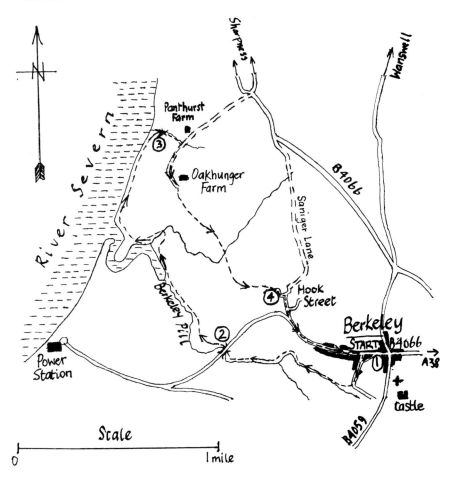

Scale

0 _____ 1 mile

Route 9   4½ miles
Round and about Berkeley

START   *Berkeley. The town stands at the junction of the B4066 and the B4509, two miles west of the A38. Park near the town centre. O.S. Sheets Landranger 162 (Gloucester & Forest of Dean) and Outdoor Leisure 14 (Wye Valley & Forest of Dean). G.R. 684993.*

ROUTE

1. *Walk down the road signposted to the Power Station. Turn left along Stock Lane. Just before reaching Berkeley Pill (the local name for a stream), turn right by a cottage to cross a stile in a fence. (A yellow arrow denotes the route). The Power Station is now straight ahead. Follow the track between the stream and a playground. This continues as a footpath by the stream, passing gardens on the right and crossing a bridge and fields before swinging right to cross a road at a bridge.*

2. *The walk continues as the Severn Way Path alongside the stream for a short way before following a raised bank to the right. Cross stiles and continue towards the Severn, passing a bridge on the left which leads to the Power Station. Keep Berkeley Pill on your left. The path swings right and the cranes and dockside buildings of Sharpness can be seen ahead. Keep on as far as a gated bridge on the right.*

3. *Cross this bridge and go over 2 fields through gates to reach a lane. Turn right along it to pass Oakhunger Farm on your left. Just before the farm track swings to the left, turn right through a gateway (electric fence warning notice on a post) and keep a hedge on the left across a large field. Leave the field by the left-hand of 2 gates at the far corner, to follow a bridle lane as far as a road. (Hook Street).*

4. *Turn right, then left to return to Berkeley.*

ACCESS BY BUS
Badgerline Ltd. (No. 308) from Bristol and Gloucester.

43

hut in the garden where he carried out many of his experiments, is strongly recommended.

Nearby stands the parish church - a rarity on account of its separate tower. Inside, among other things, can be seen Jenner's tomb. He died at the age of 74 in 1823 and there is also a memorial to him in Gloucester Cathedral.

Refreshments   There is a choice of inns in Berkeley. Refreshments can also be obtained at the castle (Tuesdays to Saturdays during the summer months).

MAY HILL

May Hill

Outline   Glasshouse ~ Newent Woods (footpath) ~ May Hill ~ Yew Tree Inn, Cliffords Mesne ~ Newent Woods (road) ~ Glasshouse.

Summary   A climb through dense woodland, a gentle ascent of a breezy hilltop, sweeping views across a dozen counties and a short stretch of level road walking through more woodland - few walks of little over 3 miles in length can compare with this for variety. Add to all that the changing pageant of seasonal wild life - trees, flowers, birds, insects - and here is a walk totally unlike any other across the whole of Gloucestershire - a walk for all the family to look back on with enjoyment and a sense of satisfaction.

Attractions   Rising to 971 feet above sea level, the pine-topped summit of May Hill is one of Gloucestershire's most prominent landmarks. 'May Hill contrasts well with the long and silvery reaches of the Severn', wrote the clergyman-diarist Francis Witts in 1823. A century later, the Poet Laureate, John Masefield, captured in verse the sight of a solitary ploughman on the flank of the hill:

> 'Ploughing the hill with steady yoke
> Of pine trees lightning-struck and broke.
> I've marked the May Hill ploughman stay
> There on his hill, day after day,
> Driving his team against the sky.'

The pines that we see today, creaking and groaning in the wind's blast, were planted to commemorate Queen Victoria's Golden Jubilee in 1887, replacing the older trees that John Masefield described. They too, will be succeeded in time by the plantations of young trees growing nearby. While children search for the commemorative plaque and the Ordnance Survey pillar, adults will feast their eyes on the spectacular view, encompassing the Malverns, the Forest of Dean, the Vale of Severn, with the river's sweeping bends, the Cotswold scarp, and in the far distance westwards, the Brecon Beacons and the plateau of the Welsh mountains.

Once known as Yartleton Hill, May Hill owes its present name to an old May Day custom, in which parties of young local people enacted a play about Summer driving away Winter. After the mock battle between the seasons, the participants carried off branches and wild flowers back to their villages.

continued on page 48

Route 10

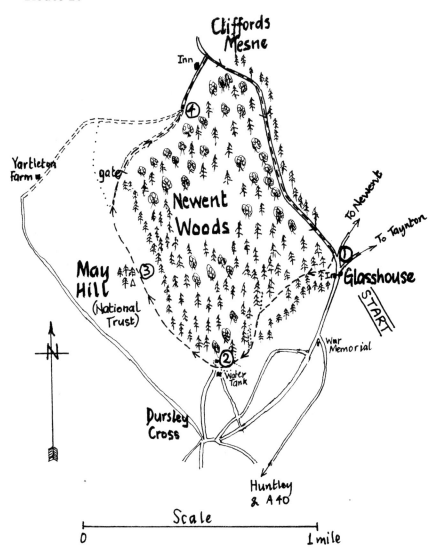

Clifords Mesne

Inn

Yartleton Farm

gate

④

Newent Woods

To Newent

To Taynton

①

← Inn Glasshouse

START

May Hill
(National Trust)

③

War Memorial

②

Water Tank

Dursley Cross

N

Huntley & A40

Scale

0   1 mile

Route 10   3¼ miles

May Hill

START   *The hamlet of Glasshouse, 1¼ miles N.W. of Huntley, reached from the A40 between Huntley and Lea. Approaching from Huntley and Gloucester, watch for a turning on the right, signposted 'Glasshouse 1¼'. At a junction with a war memorial on the left, turn right along a road signposted to Newent and Dymock. The road descends to Glasshouse. Park on the left just beyond the Glasshouse Inn on the right. O.S. Sheets Landranger 162 (Gloucester & Forest of Dean) and Pathfinder 1065 (Ross-on-Wye East). G.R. 709214.*

ROUTE

1. *Follow the road signposted Cliffords Mesne. Just beyond a road on the right to Newent, cross a stile on the left in a wire fence. Climb the track into Newent Woods. The track soon becomes a footpath. Ignore side turns. Eventually the path swings to the right to join a track. Turn left along it and climb to reach a crossroads of tracks in a clearing. Cross over, keeping woodland on the right and, still ignoring side tracks, climb to the top of a slope. Here, 5 tracks meet, with open views away to the left and a white building visible on the left below. Turn left and descend to reach the top of a lane with a water tank on the left.*

2. *Take the second turn on the right and climb past a National Trust sign and a barrier to go through a hand gate on to May Hill. The tree clump on the summit is straight ahead.*

3. *To continue the walk, leave the trees and go down through a gate on the right at the left-hand edge of woodland. Keep straight on down the clear track to join a road just before a cattle grid.*

4. *Turn right down this road. The Yew Tree Inn is on the left near the foot of the slope. From the inn, continue down to the junction and turn right for the last stretch of the walk through Newent Woods back to Glasshouse.*

Leaving the hill to the sheep, the descent from the common down to the Yew Tree Inn is enlivened by grazing ponies, noted for their tameness. The common also offers plenty of bird life, including pheasants, green woodpeckers and the occasional hovering kestrel. The old birch trees bear two distinctive growths - a gall known as witch's broom and a white bracket fungus called razor strop on account of its former use for sharpening cut-throat razors.

Back in the hamlet of Glasshouse, two features are worth noticing. One in the inn sign, depicting glassblowers at work - a reminder of how a former local industry gave the place its name. The other is the excellent example of topiary across the road, in the form of a cottage.

Refreshments The Yew Tree Inn, Cliffords Mesne. Lunches. Bar meals. The Glasshouse Inn. Bar snacks.

DYMOCK CHURCH

The Daffodil Way to Dymock

Outline   Queen's Wood car park ~ Kempley Green ~ Dymock Wood ~ Boyce Court ~ Dymock ~ Allum's Farm ~ New Grange ~ Kempley Green ~ Queen's Wood car park.

Summary   Like the May Hill route, this walk is somewhat out of place in a collection of south Gloucestershire rambles. It is set in the quiet north-west country close to the Herefordshire border, and the character of the landscape reflects its position. Despite its out-of-the-way location however, it deserves inclusion for it offers the enterprising family a pleasant day's ramble in an area rich in wild flowers, especially daffodils, and famous for its association with a group of poets.

Attractions   It was in 1988 that the Windcross Public Paths Project created the Daffodil Way, an 8-mile waymarked circular walk in an area of Gloucestershire in which many footpaths have fallen into disuse. This route follows much of the Daffodil Way, so called because of the once-prolific wild daffodils that grew in the locality. Between March and early May, these delightful flowers still gladden the steps, although their numbers have diminished considerably in recent years. This decline is not thought to have been caused by over-picking, but by the expansion of modern farming methods, which are responsible for the loss of many of our wild flowers.

A century or so ago, the daffodils were so numerous that they were gathered in great quantities and sent by the trainload for sale in Birmingham and other large cities. Even as late as the early years of the present century, the wild daffodils - smaller and paler than their cultivated relatives - were so common that Lascelles Abercrombie, a poet who came to live in the area, described them as 'Running in golden tides' towards his house at Ryton Firs.

Abercrombie was not the only poet to find this area a pleasant one in which to live. During the years leading up to the First World War, several other poets - among them Wilfrid Gibson, Edward Thomas and Robert Frost - settled nearby, and were visited by their poet friends. In Dymock church can be seen an exhibition of their work, and a collection of books, photographs, and other items associated with Dymock's brief period of fame.

Families following the route in summer and autumn will see many other wild flowers to compensate for the passing of the daffodils. In

continued on page 52

49

Route 11

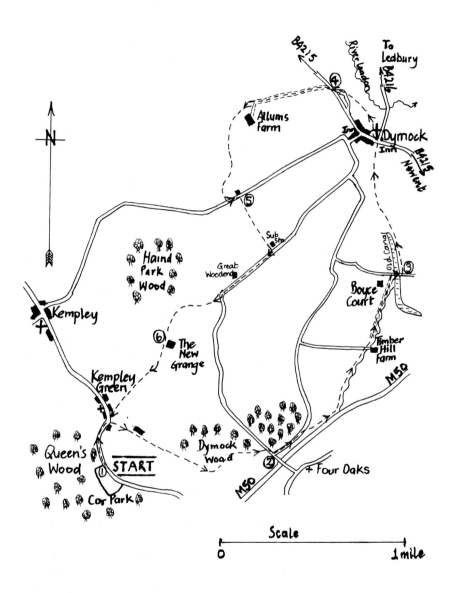

Route 11   6¼ miles

The Daffodil Way to Dymock

START   *Queen's Wood car park (Forestry Commission), ½ mile south of Kempley Green, on the minor road linking Newent, Kempley and Much Marcle. O.S. Sheet Landranger 149 (Hereford & Leominster). G.R. 677286.*

ROUTE

1. *Walk up the road towards Kempley Green, which soon comes into view ahead. Just beyond a bungalow, Knapp View, turn right and right again to follow a signposted footpath, marked with yellow arrows and black dots. This path crosses a stile by the side of the bungalow and keeps a hedge on the left. It then climbs past barns before dipping along an avenue of pear trees to enter an orchard by a field gate. Keep on the same line and enter Dymock Wood over a stile. Follow the yellow arrows through the wood. Pass a barrier and turn right along a road.*

2. *Just before the bridge over the M50, turn left along a road parallel to the motorway. (Beware of local traffic - difficult to hear). When this road swings to the left, keep straight on through a field gate. Continue in the same direction through 2 more gates to reach a tree-lined stream. Turn left along it and follow it, crossing a farm track via 2 stiles. Now keep a hedge on the right and go through a field gate to reach a track. Turn left and follow it towards Boyce Court, passing a pond and a derelict canal on the right, to reach a road at a bridge. Turn right over it and then immediately left over a stile.*

3. *Keep the canal on the left and cross a footbridge. Dymock church can now be seen ahead. The path keeps hedges on the right through 2 fields, crosses a stile, passes through an orchard and climbs up to the village. The walk continues through the churchyard. From the porch, turn left to pass round the tower. Walk along an avenue of lime trees, keeping straight on at a bend, to leave the churchyard through a kissing gate. Take the left-hand of 2 signposted paths and cross the field to a footbridge. Turn left up the next field, aiming for the de-restriction signs visible on the road ahead. Cross a stile and turn right along a service road to reach the main road.*

4. *Cross carefully and take the track towards Allums Farm. When the track bends to the left, keep straight on over a wire fence. Cross another similar fence by the end of a barn and, turning left to pass a trough, aim for a gate in the hedge ahead. Enter an orchard and turn right. Leave by a stile at the top left hand corner. Keep a fence on the left up a field to*

51

reach a road through a gate. Turn left and, in 150 metres, turn right through a gate opposite farm buildings.

5. Follow the wide grassy track, passing an electricity sub-station on the left, to reach a road. Turn right. Beyond a house with a pond on the right (Great Woodend) take a signposted footpath, also on the right, through a red gate. Climb up the middle of the field to cross a stile. Cross 2 fields to enter a farmyard (The New Grange) by a gate.

6. Keep to the right, following the yellow arrows. After passing through a gate, climb to the top left-hand corner of a steep irregular field. Go through the left-hand of 2 gates and keep right with a hedge on the right. Go through a gate and, with a hedge on the left, reach a grassy track leading to the bungalow passed on the outward stage of the walk. Turn left along the road back to the start.

Dymock Wood can be found centaury, yellow pimpernel, betony and enchanter's nightshade. The insect life includes several species of butterfly, such as speckled wood, large skipper and comma. The activities of wood ants are well worth studying - one colony had used pine needles for the building of their anthill, while another hill was comprised of the sheaths of beech buds. Watch out too, for dragonflies when passing alongside the stretch of abandoned canal near Boyce Court.

Refreshments Beauchamp Arms, Dymock. Bar meals. Crown Inn, Dymock. Bar meals.

BEECH

North Nibley and the Cotswold Way

Outline   Old London Road, Wotton ~ Westridge Wood ~ North Nibley ~ Forthay ~ Nibley Knoll (Tyndale monument) ~ Brackenbury Ditches ~ Westridge Wood ~ Old London Road.

Summary   This is a short but challenging walk over some of the finest scenic countryside in south Gloucestershire. Families with young children may wish to reduce the distance - and the challenge -by taking a picnic and omitting the North Nibley section of the walk (3) and (4) altogether. (There is an excellent wooded dell picnic place on the route). Otherwise, be prepared for a steep descent to the village and a stiff climb back!

Attractions   Fine woods, glorious views, the site of a prehistoric fort, a landmark commemorating a great man - all of these can be enjoyed on this short walk, much of which is routed along the Cotswold Way, a 100-mile waymarked long distance footpath from Bath to Chipping Campden.

Whatever the time of year, Cotswold woodlands offer delights in plenty for all the family. Beech and ash are the commonest broadleaved trees encountered, with larch the most abundant conifer. In spring, the way is carpeted with dogs mercury, wood anemones and primroses, to be followed as the year advances by a succession of colourful wayside flowers. Resident bird life includes several species of tit, goldcrest and treecreeper, supplemented from spring onwards by chiffchaff, willow warbler and blackcap.

Emerging from the woods, an awe-inspiring sight awaits. From the topograph, older children will enjoy identifying such features as the Severn Bridge (12 miles) and Oldbury power station (8 miles), while parents may well wish to pick out, with the aid of a map and binoculars, other prominent features from this superb vantage point.

Having admired the view, older children will readily appreciate why Nibley Knoll was chosen as the site for the Tyndale monument, a landmark for many miles around. It was erected in 1866 in remembrance of the life and work of William Tyndale, who translated the New Testament into English and who was martyred at Vilorde, in Flanders, in 1536. Tradition has it that Tyndale was born at North Nibley in 1484. This distinctive viewing tower stands 111 feet high and is 26½ feet square. It is of course kept locked but the key can be obtained from the village (see the notice at (3).

continued on page 56

Route 12

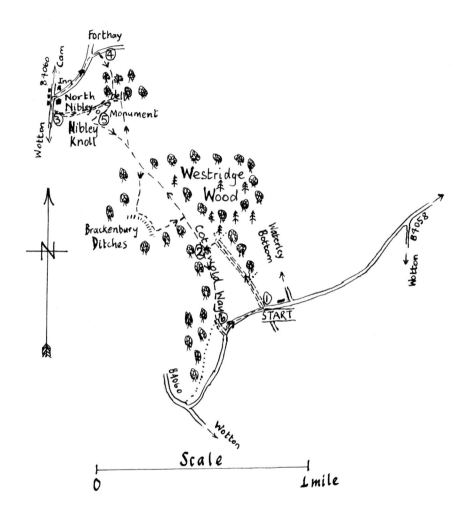

Route 12   4¼ miles
North Nibley and the Cotswold Way

START   *The old London Road, 1 mile north of Wotton-under-Edge.*
Approaching from Wotton, take the B4060 (Dursley) and in ¼ mile,
turn sharp right up the hill indicated as unsuitable for heavy vehicles.
Approaching from Tetbury along the B4058, watch for a right turn
indicated as unsuitable for heavy vehicles opposite a golf course and just
after a low gear sign. Park on the verge opposite derelict farm buildings
near a lane signposted Waterley Bottom. O.S. Sheet Landranger 162
(Gloucester & Forest of Dean). G.R. 757944.

ROUTE

Walk along the road in the direction of Wotton. Pass a footpath signposted
Coombe Hill and a lane on the left, to reach a track signposted Tyndale
Monument.

1. *Turn right along the track. Keep woodland on the right as far as a*
   5-ways junction. Take the left-hand track to reach a T-junction.

2. *Turn right and keep to the right along the Cotswold Way (marked with*
   yellow arrows and white dots). Soon after the Tyndale Monument
   comes into view on the left, at a point where the Cotswold Way veers
   sharply left, take instead the descending path on the left immediately
   beyond. Eventually this path veers to the left and climbs before
   dropping through a wooded dell and descending to North Nibley along
   a wide track.

3. *At the bottom, turn right along the road into the village. The Black*
   Horse Inn is on the right at the junction with Barrs Lane. To continue
   the walk, keep on along Barrs Lane. At Forthay, keep right at a road
   fork (signposted Millend). In a short distance, cross a stile on the right.

4. *Follow the steeply climbing footpath, keeping a hedge on the left. The*
   Tyndale Monument can be seen above the trees to the right. Enter
   woodland over a stile and continue climbing to reach the dell passed
   through earlier. Cross straight over and go over a stile into a grassy
   quarry floor. Keep to the right, round the edge, to cross another stile.
   Now follows a rather difficult climb over rocks to reach a last stile, from
   which a path leads directly to the Tyndale Monument.

5. *From the monument, veer to the left, following the Cotswold Way along*
   the escarpment, and keeping a fence on the right, Pass a topograph and
   enter woodland to arrive, via a stile, at a junction passed earlier. Retrace
   the outward route for a short way by turning right. In 100 metres, bear
   right at a fork, leaving the Cotswold Way. The path eventually climbs up

past Brackenbury Ditches to rejoin the Way. Here, bear right along it as far as the next junction, passed earlier (2). Instead of turning left and retracing, follow the Cotswold Way to the end of Westridge Wood.

6. *Here a lane on the left leads back to the road from which the walk began. Turn left along it back to the start.*

ACCESS BY BUS
Circle Line Coaches connect Wotton with Dursley and Gloucester. Stroud Valley Buses link Wotton with Dursley and Stroud.

––––––

From late May onwards the unimproved limestone grassland around the monument and in the old quarry nearby are ideal places to search for wild flowers. With the aid of a pocket flora, such species as early purple orchid, rock rose, salad burnet and yellow hawkweed can all be identified. These flowers in turn attract several species of butterflies, especially the common blue and the small skipper.

An added attraction on an autumn walk in this area are the luscious blackberries along the stretch between Westridge Wood and the monument.

Families possessing a kite may like to take advantage of Nibley Knoll's excellent aspect.

Refreshments   Black Horse Inn, North Nibley. Restaurant. Bar meals. Garden.

MINCHINHAMPTON

Cotswold Commons around Minchinhampton

Outline   Burleigh ~ Besbury Common ~ Minchinhampton ~ the
Bulwarks ~ Minchinhampton Common ~ Burleigh.

Summary   This walk is centred around the ancient little Cotswold wool
town of Minchinhampton and much of the route is over common land -
unfenced areas of hill country scattered with the remains of prehistoric
activity. The views from these open grassland areas are some of the best
in the south Cotswolds and the feeling of spaciousness and freedom to
roam will not be lost on children. A word of warning - Minchinhampton
Common is intersected by several roads -and don't forget the hazard of
goif balls!

Attractions   The 580-acre Minchinhampton Common is the second-
largest common in Gloucestershire (Cleeve Common being the largest).
Contrary to popular belief, less than a quarter of our surviving commons
have public right of access. As the common land walked over on this route
is owned by the National Trust, it is not only safeguarded for public
recreation but it is also preserved from agricultural use or building
development.

Commons were originally land reserved for the grazing of stock and
the gathering of firewood. Today, they are valuable for their wild life, and
grassland flowers, together with butterflies, are highlights of summer
walks.

Minchinhampton Common has its share of mysteries, too. The vast
earthworks known as the Bulwarks still continue to puzzle archaeologists
and historians. They are believed to date from the Iron Age (possibly
from about 100 A.D.) and to have been built for defence but their
arrangement is unlike that of other defensive earthworks. Children will
lose no time in devising their own uses for these strange structures. Other
earthworks on the route, near Amberley, are the remains of a hill fort,
dating from a similar period to the Bulwarks.

The Common is an ideal area for kite and model-aircraft flying.
Minchinhampton today is little larger than a big village but was once one
of the most famous of the Cotswold cloth-manufacturing towns. Many of
its buildings retain their prosperous appearance, a good example being
the Market House, which dates from 1698. It stands on stone columns
with additional wooden supports. By craning their necks, older children
will be able to read the 'Scale of Charges', high up on one of the walls.

continued on page 60

57

Route 13

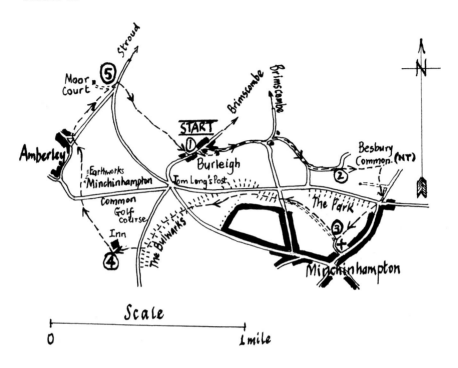

Scale

0   1 mile

COMMON BLUE, MALE

Route 13   4¼ miles
Cotswold Commons around Minchinhampton

START *At Burleigh. Leave Stroud along the A419 (towards Cirencester). In 3 miles, at Brimscombe, turn right along a road signposted 'Burleigh ¼ Minchinhampton 1½'. After climbing steeply and crossing a cattle grid, watch out for a lane on the left immediately beyond a bus stop, alongside which are a phone and a postbox. Park on the verge. O.S. Sheets Landranger 162 (Gloucester and Forest of Dean) and Pathfinder 1113 (Stroud). G.R. 862015.*

ROUTE
1. *Follow the lane, which soon narrows to path width. At a T-junction in front of Clowder House, turn left along a descending path to reach a road. Turn right along it. At a junction, bear left to pass Burleigh House. Keep straight on, ignoring a left turn, following a narrow lane. Beyond a sign indicating Love Lane, keep left at a junction to reach Besbury Common (National Trust).*

2. *Keep the wall on the right and cross 2 stiles. At a signpost, turn right over a V-shaped stile into a field. Cross a drive by 2 stiles and then go over a small field to reach a narrow road. Turn right along it to reach a road junction on the edge of Minchinhampton. Cross to reach the Common (Great Park - National Trust). Now follow the wall on the left with Minchinhampton church ahead. Those wishing to visit the town (and/or the Crown Inn) should keep straight on past the small grassy circle on the edge of the Common.*

3. *Resuming the walk from the grassy circle, follow the line of the wall bordering the private road, swinging to the left with it to cross Dr. Brown's Road and reach the Bulwarks (a system of ancient earthworks). Keep straight on, still with the wall on the left, passing the gateways to Seymour House and Westfield. Beyond Westfield, where the wall veers left, keep straight on, aiming for the right-hand side of a tree clump ahead. Cross a road to pass Windmill House and continue along the Bulwarks until they almost meet a road on the right. At this point, cross the road and make for the left-hand corner of the wall enclosing the Old Lodge Inn and the golf clubhouse.*

4. *From the corner, strike off to the right across the Common, with a wooded valley on the left, aiming in the direction of houses amidst trees ahead (Amberley). Cross a road just above Amberley and, aiming for a gap to the left of the house on the far right ahead, climb past earthworks*

to reach a road junction. Pass a war memorial and keep right, following the road to its junction with the Stroud-Cirencester road.

5. *Cross this busy road and aim half-right for Burleigh, which appears as a group of houses in the trees below the Common. Eventually, on approaching a house with a battlemented turret, bear right to meet a road, reached almost opposite a 'No through road' sign. Turn left down the busy road back to the start.*

ACCESS BY BUS
Rover European Travel buses connect Minchinhampton with Chalford and Cirencester.

Stroud Valley buses connect with Stroud and Nailsworth.

Nearby stands Holy Trinity church, with its unusual truncated spire. The top was removed in 1563 and replaced by the stone coronet we see today. Inside can be seen many fine tomb brasses, including one in memory of one of Gloucestershire's most famous sons, John Bradley, who became Astronomer Royal, and who died in 1762.

Children with boundless energy may be persuaded to make a short diversion near the end of the walk to see Tom Long's Post. This 6-fingered signpost is reputed to have marked the grave of a highwayman executed nearby.

Refreshments Crown Inn, Minchinhampton. Lunches and bar meals. Old Lodge Inn, Minchinhampton Common. Bar meals. Garden.

OWLPEN MANOR

60

Route 14   4 miles

Owlpen and Uley Bury

Outline   First Section: Uley ~ Owlpen ~ Uley.
Second Section: Uley ~ Uley Bury ~ Uley.

Summary   This walk starts at Uley, one of the more attractive of the larger south Cotswold villages, and proceeds over fields to Owlpen, a gem among the smaller ones. Hopefully, the striking views of Uley Bury on the return route of this short walk will spur the family to tackle the stiff climb up to this Iron Age hillfort and in so doing, complete a walk of rich diversity with plenty to interest the young and not-so-young alike.

Attractions   Uley is a long straggling village well worth exploring. It contains many handsome Georgian houses - evidence of its past prosperity as a cloth-manufacturing centre. Its most notable product was 'Uley Blue' - a high-quality cloth which, together with 'Stroud Scarlet' - was made into military uniforms in the days when army regiments dressed in fine apparel. Although the present church is Victorian, several tabletop tombs of wealthy 18th century cloth manufacturers can be seen in the churchyard. Owlpen, by contrast, is a tiny place consisting of manor house, church, and a few scattered farms. The view of the medieval manor, with the church and woods in the background, is one of the most admired in the entire Cotswolds and can be enjoyed by going a short way along the track to the right after turning into the hamlet from the footpath.

     Like Uley church, that at Owlpen is a 19th century re-building. It is however, decorated in the Pre-Raphaelite style. Children may like to search in the churchyard for a most realistically-modelled giant fly on a tombstone.

     For those who prefer their wild life in the natural state, this walk offers rewards in plenty. The lake passed on the approach to Owlpen has its resident mallard and moorhens. Large flocks of gulls often forage in the fields, while the steep banks on either side of the lane winding up to Owlpen Farm are rich in ferns and lime-loving wild flowers.

     The 32-acre Iron Age hill fort of Uley Bury is the most spectacular in Gloucestershire. It dates from around 300 B.C. and was defended by terracing and an embankment, with entrances at the north, south and east corners. The actual fort is in private ownership but the walk round the ramparts, as well as giving magnificent views in all directions, reveals how

continued on page 64

61

Route 14

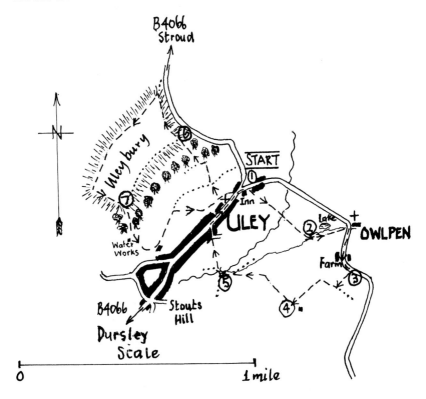

MALLARD

Route 14   4 miles

(or 2 short walks, each of 2 miles)

Owlpen and Uley Bury

START   *Uley. The village green, opposite the church. Uley lies on the B4066 between Stroud and Dursley. Park in the village. O.S. Sheet Landranger 162 (Gloucester & Forest of Dean). G.R. 793986.*

ROUTE - Owlpen section.

1. *Follow the gravelled drive alongside Pink Cottage, close to the Old Crown Inn. The drive continues as a footpath between gardens before descending to a stile. Go down a sloping field and cross a stream by stepping stones to another stile. Bear right in the next field, as indicated by the yellow arrow, and climb to cross a stiled footbridge.*

2. *Now bear left alongside the stream, passing a lake on the left, to reach a road over a stile. Turn left into Owlpen. After seeing the manor house and church, retrace steps as far as the stile crossed earlier. Keep straight on up the lane, passing Owlpen Farm. Just before a left-hand bend, cross a stile on the right (with a dog gate alongside).*

3. *Cross a field, keeping a fence on the right. Cross a stile and descend a sloping field to another stile with a dog gate. In the next field, go half-left to cross a stile near an ash tree. The next stile is straight ahead in a ranch fence and, from here, the path passes a power pole and proceeds to the corner of a field with a farm on the left above.*

4. *Turn right, down the hedge side to cross a double stile into another field. Take a diagonal course to cross a stile and the right-hand of 2 footbridges in the bottom left-hand corner.*

5. *Turn right and climb the grassy slope ahead. Cross a stile by bungalow gardens and follow the path to the village street. Turn right back to the start.*

ROUTE - Uley Bury section

Take the footpath marked 'Uley Bury & Whitecourt' alongside the churchyard. Turn right by a bungalow (Hillcroft) and climb to a stile. Keep on the same line up a steep field towards woodland. Turn left along the woodland fringe as far as a handgate. Go through and continue climbing, passing a metal fence on the right, to reach a stile by a gate. Beyond, keep on along the path, which soon scales the ramparts of the bury.

6. *Turn right along the level path round the perimeter of the enclosure and follow it along 3 sides of its rectangular shape, to reach the southern corner of the bury. (Those wishing to walk the complete perimeter can do so and then retrace their steps to this point).*

7. *To return to Uley, take the path to the right, descending through woodland. (Care needed - steep gradient and loose stones). Ignore all right turns and keep on down to a stile by a gate, beyond which the path leaves the wood to drop past a water works and reach a metalled track. Below, by a house, follow the footpath signposted to the church. This passes a children's playground and skirts gardens before joining the path walked earlier by the churchyard. Retrace the short distance back to the start.*

ACCESS BY BUS
Uley is on the Stroud - Dursley service (Stroud Valley buses).

---

cleverly the Iron Age builders made use of the natural contours in constructing a fortress capable of sheltering up to 2,000 people. A mile north of Uley Bury is the famous chambered long barrow known as the Uley tumulus, or Hetty Pegler's Tump. This can be seen by parking at a layby off the B4066. The key can be obtained from a cottage on the way up the hill from Uley.

Refreshments The Old Crown Inn, Uley. Lunches. Bar snacks. Garden.

DRAGONFLY

Cotswold Water Park

Outline   Spine Road car park ~ Wildmoorway Lane ~ Thames &
Severn Canal ~ Cerney Wick ~ old railway ~ Spine Road car park.

Summary   This is an easy walk, flat throughout its length, yet full of
interest. The Cotswold Water Park is a complex of artificial lakes created
as a result of gravel extraction. This industry is still active in the area and
care should be taken to keep to the clearly-defined paths. These paths are
chiefly along a dismantled railway and the towpath of a long-derelict
canal and as the old railway stretch is classified as a bridleway, walkers
may well encounter horse-riders along this section of the route.

Attractions   The Cotswold Water Park is intended to provide a range of
leisure activities, several of which can be seen along the route. These
include sailing, angling, water sports, jet ski-ing and a sailboard school.
Near Somerford Keynes, a few miles to the west, are a country park and a
nature reserve.

Nowhere in Gloucestershire has the rural landscape undergone so
much change in such a short time as here. Two hundred years ago, a
29-mile-long canal linking the rivers Thames and Severn was dug through
what was then quiet farming country. Although the canal had leakage
problems from the start, it must have made a considerable impact on the
lives of the local people. Within a century however, a new form of
transport and communication had arrived. This was the railway, built to
connect Cirencester with Swindon. It quickly robbed the canal of trade
and made its own indelible mark on the landscape.

By 1961 however, both canal and railway had ceased to operate. By
this time, gravel-digging had commenced and since then the novel
concept of a leisure park based on flooded and landscaped gravel pits has
become a reality and transformed the area.

The car park from which the walk starts retains a reminder of the
days of steam trains. This is the old railway bridge, wisely spared from
demolition to serve as a link with the not-too-distant past. Keen eyes will
spot the bat box beneath the bridge - placed there by conservationists to
provide a much-needed breeding site for these interesting flying
mammals. The canal too, though largely overgrown, still keeps two
features dating from its construction in the 1780s. These are the lock and
the round house near Cerney Wick - the one intended to conserve water
as the canal negotiated uneven ground, the other built to provide the
lock-keeper with a distinctively designed home.

continued on page 68

65

Route 15

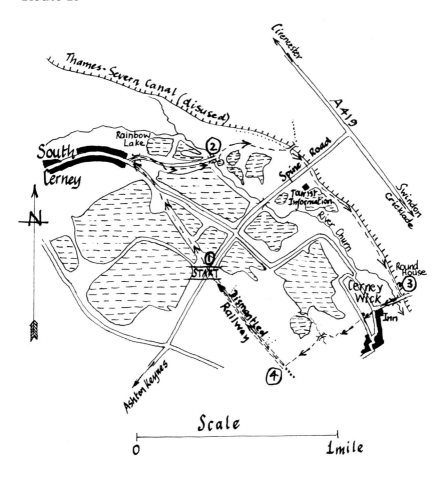

Route 15 3¾ miles

Cotswold Water Park

START *Car park by old railway bridge off Spine Road, a mile west of the A419, and a mile south east of South Cerney. O.S. Sheets Landranger 163 (Cheltenham & Cirencester) and Pathfinder 1134. G.R. 064963.*

ROUTE

1. *Leave the car park through a handgate on the right, following the signpost indicating 'South Cerney Lakes'. This path follows the course of the old railway. On reaching a road, turn left along it as far as Wildmoorway Lane on the right. This is signposted Cerney Wick. Follow the lane, crossing the old railway bridge and passing Rainbow Lake on your left. In 70 metres, climb a stile on the right to take the footpath parallel to the road, keeping the lake on the right. Cross another stile and eventually reach the road walked along earlier at a bridge.*

2. *Now take the path signposted 'Information Layby'. Soon, this path crosses a stile and continues along a track bordered by hedges. Cross one stile and, on reaching a second leading over the old canal at a derelict lock, do not cross but turn right along the footpath signposted Cerney Wick. Cross Spine Road (the Information Centre is on the right) and after climbing a stile, keep left to follow the canal towpath. Cross a concrete bridge and ignore a path on the right leading to the River Churn. Instead, keep straight on along the towpath to meet a road at a lock with a round house nearby.*

3. *Turn right along the road, crossing the River Churn by a bridge. On reaching a T-junction by the Crown Inn, keep straight on over a stile and cross a field to another stile leading to a road by a cottage. The path crosses the road and more fields by means of stiles to reach a lake. Keep the lake on your right as far as a sharp right corner, at which point the path, marked by a yellow arrow and white spot, turns left from the lake side. Follow it, crossing a footbridge and keeping a hedge on the left across a large field to meet a wide path (the track of the old railway).*

4. *Turn right along this path and, ignoring side turns, keep straight on to cross Spine Road once more and arrive back at the starting point.*

ACCESS BY BUS
Buses connect the Cotswold Water Park with Cirencester, Swindon, Malmesbury and Cricklade.

Wildlife interest abounds on this walk. Trout can be seen swimming in the water alongside the path, dragonflies are abundant in the summer sunshine, and great crested grebes, coots, moorhens, reed buntings and sedge warblers all find the reedy fringes of the lake ideal habitat.

Refreshments   The Crown Inn, Cerney Wick. Bar meals.

HALFPENNY BRIDGE, LECHLADE

Route 16

The Thames at Lechlade

Outline   Lechlade ~ Coln-Thames confluence ~ Halfpenny Bridge ~ St. John's Lock and Bridge ~ Lechlade.

Summary   This short easy route along the Thames valley to the south of Lechlade offers a gentle introduction to riverside walking. Despite its shortness, the route if full of scenic, historical and natural history appeal, with the little town of Lechlade, whose fine church spire is visible throughout much of the walk, providing additional interest at the end.

Attractions   The name of 'Old Father Thames' has a magical ring to it and a walk along this most familiar of rivers cannot fail to appeal to children. 'Thames or Isis' proclaims the map about this stretch of river upstream from Oxford, and to children who have seen the Thames flowing majestically through London, the modest stream followed here presents a striking contrast.

Indeed, the walk provides a unique opportunity to see the Thames swelled by the waters of 3 of its tributary rivers. The confluence with the Coln is passed early in the walk, while from St. John's Bridge can be seen the last reaches of the Cole, flowing north from Wiltshire, and the Leach, which gave its name both to Northleach and to Lechlade itself.

Lechlade is Gloucestershire's only town on the Thames and as such has a long history. Its two bridges are worth inspecting. The first encountered, Halfpenny Bridge, was so called because of the toll once charged to cross. It was built in 1792 and the toll house can still be seen. St. John's Bridge is much older. It was first built in the 14th century but was twice widened and improved during the last century.

The statue of Father Thames by St. John's Lock was made for the Great Exhibition held at the Crystal Palace, London, in 1851. It was later re-erected at the source of the Thames, near Kemble, but was removed to its present place in 1974 to protect it from vandalism.

The canal and round house passed early in the walk were built 200 years ago. The canal was the Thames and Severn (walked along on Route 15) - a 29-mile-long waterway linking our two largest rivers. Derelict now, this canal had structural problems from the start but it brought more trade to Lechlade, which was already a busy port, with riverside wharves at which local cheeses and other farm products were loaded for shipment to London.

continued on page 72

Route 16

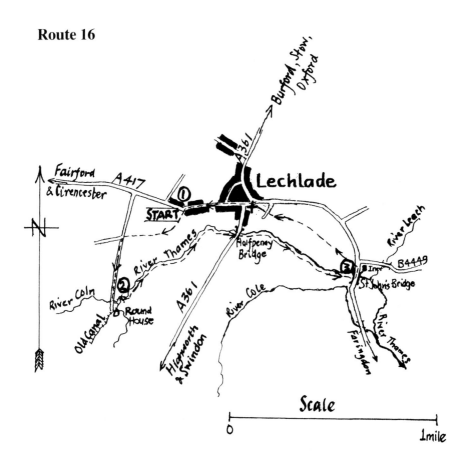

Scale

0   1mile

Route 16   3¼ miles

The Thames at Lechlade

START   *Lechlade. The town stands at the junction of the A417 and the A361, 13 miles east of Cirencester. Park as near as possible to the town centre. O.S. Sheet Landranger 163 (Cheltenham and Cirencester area). G.R. 215995.*

ROUTE

Walk along the A417 towards Fairford and Cirencester. Just beyond a service road on the left, watch out for a signpost indicating a public footpath.

1. *Cross the concrete stile. After a second stile, the path crosses fields by way of 4 stiled footbridges, with the River Thames away to the left. After crossing another stile, the path reaches a lane at a bend. Keep on along this lane for 20 metres before turning left along a private road (public footpath). Go over one cattle grid and, immediately before a second, leave the road to take the footpath on the left, which follows the River Coln on the last short stretch of its journey to meet the Thames.*

2. *Cross the footbridge over the Thames, noticing the entrance to the derelict Thames - Severn Canal on the right, together with the associated round house. Follow the Thames-side path towards Lechlade church. On reaching Halfpenny Bridge, pass under the small arch and continue along the river bank as far as St. John's Lock. The statue of Father Thames can be seen outside the lock-keeper's house.*

3. *Leave the river here by climbing up to the road and turning left over St. John's Bridge. After passing the Trout Inn on the right, watch out for a metalled footpath on the left, opposite the B4449 junction. This path leads back to Lechlade, passing the school and crossing a road to arrive at the town centre through the churchyard.*

Lechlade had lost its former trade but discovered a new kind of prosperity - tourism. Pleasure boats keep the river - and the town -busy throughout the spring and summer months.

But for those families who want to get away from the crowds, the infant Thames has plenty of quiet stretches too. Here, coots, moorhens, and ducks dabble undisturbed and swans drift gracefully by. Dragonflies and damselflies are ceaselessly active in the sunshine, the starry flowers of water crowfoot cover the surface, and shoals of tiny fish dart in the shallows.

Refreshments The Trout Inn, St. John's Bridge. Lunches. Bar meals. Garden. Other inns in Lechlade.

TUNNEL HOUSE. Route 15.

Appendices

ROUTES IN ORDER OF DIFFICULTY

Easy walks - flat going throughout:

Route 8 - *Sharpness Canal (retracing steps)*.
Route 15 - *Cotswold Water Park*.
Route 16 - *The Thames at Lechlade*.

More strenuous walks - generally easy going but with a few gentle gradients and/or rough patches:

Route 1 - *New Fancy Forest walk*.
Route 2 - *Forest Sculpture Trail*.
Route 3 - *Soudley and Mallards Pike*.
Route 4 - *Cannop, Nagshead and Parkend*.
Route 8 - *Sharpness Canal (complete walk)*.
Route 9 - *Round and about Berkeley*.
Route 10 - *May Hill*.
Route 11 - *The Daffodil Way to Dymock*.
Route 12 - *North Nibley and the Cotswold Way (excluding North Nibley)*.
Route 13 - *Cotswold Commons around Minchinhampton*.
Route 14 - *Uley to Owlpen (only)*.

Strenuous walks - (On Gloucestershire standards), involving steep gradients and/or some rough going:

Route 5 - *Newland and Staunton Stones*.
Route 6 - *St. Briavels and Wye Valley*.
Route 7 - *Newnham and Blaize Bailey*.
Route 12 - *North Nibley and the Cotswold Way*.
Route 14 - *Owlpen and Uleybury*.

BUS OPERATORS - SOUTH AND WEST GLOUCESTERSHIRE

Operator	Area served
Applegate Coaches, Heathfield Garage, Newport, Berkeley, Glos. GL13 9PL. Tel. Dursley 260842.	Berkeley and Dursley.
Badgerline Ltd., Badger House, Oldmixon Crescent, Weston-super-Mare, Avon. BS24 9AX. Tel. Bristol 297979.	Gloucester, Bristol, Dursley, Berkeley.
K. W. Beard Ltd., Valley Road, Cinderford, Glos. GL14 2TD. Tel. Dean 23031.	Cinderford area.
Bennetts Coaches, Eastern Ave., Gloucester. GL4 7BU. Tel. Gloucester 27809.	Gloucester to Newent.
James Bevan (Lydney) Ltd., Bus Station, Hams Road, Lydney, Glos. Tel. Dean 42859.	Lydney to Gloucester.
Circle Line Coaches, Abbey Road, Monk Meadow, Gloucester. GL2 6HU. Tel. Gloucester 26662.	Wotton-under-Edge, Dursley, Berkeley, Sharpness, Gloucester.

Cottrells Coaches, Mill End,
Mitcheldean, Glos. GL17 0HP.
Tel. Dean 542224.

Cinderford, Mitcheldean,
Gloucester.

Dean Forest Coaches, Joys Green,
Lydbrook, Glos. GL17 9QU.
Tel. Dean 60346.

Cinderford and Coleford.

David Field Travel, Wheatstone House,
Watery Lane, Newent, Glos. GL18 1PY.
Tel. Newent 820979.

Ross on Wye, Newent,
Gloucester.

Newbury Coaches, Lower Road Trading Est.,
Ledbury, Herefordshire. HR8 2DJ.
Tel. Ledbury 3483.

Gloucester, Newent and
Ledbury.

Red & White (National Welsh Ltd.),
The Bulwarks, Chepstow, Gwent. NP6 5XZ.
Tel. Chepstow 3484.

Forest of Dean, Wye Valley
and Gloucester.

Rover European Travel, The Grange,
Horsley, Stroud, Glos. GL6 0PU.
Tel. Nailsworth 2722.

Chalford, Minchinhampton
and Cirencester.

Smiths Motors (Ledbury) Ltd., The Homend,
Ledbury, Herefordshire. HR8 1BA.
Tel. Ledbury 2953.

Coleford, St. Briavels,
Chepstow, Gloucester.

Soudley Valley Coaches Ltd., Soudley,
Cinderford, Glos. GL14 2TX.
Tel. Dean 22129.

Cinderford to Lydney.

Stroud Valley Buses, Bus Station,
Merrywalks, Stroud, Glos. GL5 1QA.
Tel. Stroud 763421.

Stroud, Dursley & Wotton
areas. Gloucester and
Cirencester.

Swanbrook Transport, Thomas House,
St. Margaret's Road, Cheltenham, Glos.
Tel. Cheltenham 574444.

Gloucester, Stroud and
Severnside villages.

Willetts of Yorkley, Dean Rise, Main Road,
Pillowell, Glos. GL15 4QY.
Tel. Dean 562511.

Forest of Dean, Lydney,
Gloucester.

Youngs Coaches, Newent, Glos. GL18 1PU.

Dymock, Newent, Gloucester.

WET WEATHER ALTERNATIVES - completely or partly under cover.

Museums and art galleries

    Corinium Museum, Park Street, Cirencester. Open all week. Tel. Cirencester 5611.

    Dean Heritage Museum, Soudley, Cinderford. Open daily all year. Tel. Dean (0594) 22170.

    Folk Museum & Craft Centre, Wolves Newton, nr. Chepstow. Open April-September daily, October and November, Sats. and Suns. Tel. Wolves Newton (029 15) 231.

    Gloucester Folk Museum, Bishop Hooper's Lodgings, 99-103 Westgate St., Gloucester. Open all year. Tel. Gloucester 26467.

    Gloucester Museum & Art Gallery, Brunswick Rd., Gloucester. Open all year. Mon.-Sat. and Sun. afternoons in August. Tel. Gloucester 24131.

    Gloucesters Regimental Museum, The Old Customs House, Commercial Rd., Gloucester. Open weekdays throughout year. Tel. Gloucester 22682.

    Gloucester - House of the Tailor of Gloucester, 9 College Court. Tel. Gloucester 422856.

G.W.R. Railway Museum, Coleford. Open daily except Mondays. Tel. Dean (0594) 33569.

Nature in Art, Wallsworth Hall, Sandhurst, Gloucester. Open Tues.-Suns. Tel. Gloucester 731422.

National Waterways Museum, Llanthony Warehouse, Gloucester Docks. Open daily except winter Mondays. Tel. Gloucester 25524.

Nelson Museum, Monmouth. Open all year, daily and Sun. afternoons. Tel. (0600-3519).

The Museum of Packaging & Advertising, Gloucester Docks. Open daily ex. Mondays. Tel. Gloucester 32309.

The Shambles of Newent, Museum of Victoria Life, Church St., Newent. Open Easter-Christmas. Closed Mon. ex. Bank Hol. & Christmas Day. Tel. (0531 822144).

Stroud Museum, Lansdown, Stroud. Mon.-Sat. Tel. Stroud 3394.

HISTORIC BUILDINGS

Ashleworth Tithe Barn, (N.T.), Ashleworth, nr. Gloucester. Open April-October.

Berkeley Castle and grounds, Berkeley. Open March-Sept. Oct. Sun. afternoons. Tel. (0453) 810332.

Chavenage House, nr. Tetbury. Open May-Sept. Thurs, Sun. and Bank Holiday afternoons. Tel. (0666) 52329.

Fairford church, Fairford. Fine stained glass.

Frocester Tithe Barn, Frocester Court, nr. Stonehouse. Open daily. Tel. (045382) 3250.

Gloucester Cathedral. Contains tomb of King Edward II.

Goodrich Castle, (English Heritage). 5 miles south of Ross-on-Wye. Open daily. Tel. (0600) 890538.

Hartpury Tithe Barn, nr. Gloucester. Can be viewed from outside only.

Jenner Museum, Berkeley. Open April-Sept., Tues.-Sun. and Bank Holidays. Tel. (0453) 810631.

Little Dean Hall, nr. Cinderford. Open Good Friday-end October. Tel. (0594) 24213.

Newark Park, (N.T.), Elizabethan Hunting Lodge, nr. Wotton-under-Edge. Open April, May, August and Sept. Wed. and Thurs. afternoons. Tel. (0453) 842644.

Tintern Abbey, 12 Century Cistercian Abbey. Open daily.

OTHER PLACES OF INTEREST

Beaufort Bird Gardens, Devauden Green, nr. Chepstow. Open all year. Tel. Wolves Newton (02915) 346.

Brass Rubbing Centre, Cripps Road, Cirencester. Open daily June-Sept Tel. Cirencester 3971.

Brass Rubbing Centre, The Cathedral, Gloucester. Open Mon.-Sat. July and August.

Butterfly and Natural World Centre, Birches Lane, Newent. Open Easter-end Oct. Tel. (0531) 821800.

Cirencester Park, Cirencester. Open all year.

Cotswold Water Park, nr. Cirencester. Contact The Rangers Office, Keynes Country Park, Shorncote, Cirencester. Tel. Cirencester 861459.

Clearwell Caves, near Coleford. Ancient iron mines. Open daily March-end Oct. Tel. (0594) 32535.

Dean Forest Railway (Norchard Steam Centre), nr. Lydney. Static display all year. Steam train rides Bank Hols. and Weds. and Suns. Tel. (0594) 843423.

Falconry Centre, Newent. Open Feb.-Nov. (except Tues.). Tel. (0531) 820286.

Jubilee Maze, Symonds Yat, Ross-on-Wye. Open daily April-Oct. Suns. in Nov. Tel. Symonds Yat (0600) 890360.

Lydney Park Gardens and Museums. Limited opening times, April-June. Tel. Dean (0594) 42844.

Puzzle Wood, nr. Coleford, Old iron mines. Open Easter-Oct. Closed Mon. except Bank Hol. Tel. Dean (0594) 33187.

Robinswood Hill Country Park, nr. Gloucester. Visitor Centre. Tel. Glos. 413029.

Royal Forest of Dean - Forestry Commission Information Centre. Tel. (0594) 33376.

Rural Heritage Museum, Doward, Symonds Yat. Open Easter-October. Tel. Symonds Yat 890474.

Selsley Herb & Goat Farm, Water Lane, Selsley, nr. Dursley. Open April-Sept. 6 days weekly. Tel. (04536) 6682.

Severn Wildfowl & Wetlands Trust, Slimbridge, Gloucester. Open all year. Tel. Cambridge (045389) 333.

St. Augustine's Farm. Working Farm and Country Centre, Arlingham, nr. Gloucester. Open Tues.-Sun. and Bank Hols. all year round, afternoons. Tel. Gloucester (0452) 740277.

Tintern Railway Station, Tintern, nr. Chepstow. Reconstructed station. Open Easter-October. Tel. Tintern (02918) 566.

Westbury Court Garden, (N.T.), Westbury on Severn. Rare water garden. Open April-end Oct. Wed.-Sun. and Bank Holidays. Tel. (045276) 461.

Westonbirt Arboretum, nr. Tetbury. Magnificent tree collection. Open all year.

World of Butterflies, Whitchurch, Ross on Wye. Open April-October. Nov. Sundays only. Tel. Symonds Yat (0600) 890360.

Wye Valley Open Farm, Goodrich, nr. Ross on Wye. Open Easter-end Oct. Tel. Symonds Yat (0600) 890296.

VIEWPOINTS, PICNIC SITES, ETC.

Coaley Park Picnic Site. Off B4066 between Uley and Stroud. Spectacular views. Toilets.

Haresfield Beacon. 5 miles north of Stroud. On Cotswold Way. Fine views.

Keynes Country Park. S.W. of Cirencester. Ranger's Office. Tel.(0285) 861459.

Stinchcombe Hill. 10 miles S.W. of Stroud. Superb views.

Symonds Yat, Wye Valley. Famous viewpoint. Peregrine falcon nest site.

The Severn Bore. This spectacular tidal wave can be observed from various places along the river between Sharpness and Frampton. It is best seen at the times of the Spring and Autumn tides.

USEFUL ADDRESSES AND INFORMATION

Guided walks. Cotswold Warden Service, County Planning Dept., Shire Hall, Gloucester. GL7 2TN. Tel. (0452) 425674.

Timewalk (Forest of Dean). 13 Meadow Walk, Sling, Coleford, Glos. GL16 8LR. Tel. (0594) 33544.

Wildlife. Gloucestershire Trust for Nature Conservation, Church House, Standish, Stonehouse, Glos. GL10 3EU. Tel. Stonehouse 2761.

Books and maps (Forest of Dean): The Forest Bookshop, Coleford. GL16 8AR. Tel. 0594 33858. Children's bookroom.

Youth Hostels.
Duntisbourne Abbots, near Cirencester. Tel. Miserden 682.
Shepherds Patch, Slimbridge. Tel. Cambridge (Glos.) 275.
St. Briavels Castle. Tel. Dean 530272.
Welsh Bicknor Rectory, near Ross-on-Wye. Tel. Dean 60300.

TOURIST INFORMATION CENTRES
Cinderford. The Library, Belle Vue Road. Tel. (0594) 22581.
Cirencester. Corn Hall, Market Place. Tel. (0285) 654180.
Coleford. 24 Market Place. Tel. (0594) 36307.
Gloucester. St. Michael's Tower, The Cross. Tel. (0452) 421188.
Newent. The Library, High Street. Tel. (0531) 822145.
Stroud. Subscription Rooms, Kendrick Street. Tel. (04536) 5768.
Tetbury. The Old Court House, Long Street. Tel. (0666) 53552.

LEISURE CENTRES AND SWIMMING POOLS
Berry Hill Sports Centre. Royal Forest of Dean College, Berry Hill, Coleford. Tel. (0594) 35388.
Cotswold Sports Centre. Tetbury Road, Cirencester. Tel. (0285) 654057.
Gloucester Leisure Centre. Bruton Way. Tel. (0452) 36498.
Gloucester Ski Centre. Matson Lane, Matson, Gloucester. Tel. (0452) 414300.
Heywood Sports Centre. Causeway Road, Cinderford. Tel. (0594) 24008.
Lydney Sports Centre. Sports Hall, Whitecross School, Church Road, Lydney. Tel. (0594) 842383.
Rednock Sports Centre. Rednock Drive, Dursley. Tel. 0453 3832.
St. Michael's Park. Off King Street, Cirencester. Tel. (0285) 659182.
Stratford Park Leisure Centre. Stratford Road, Stroud. Tel. (04536) 6771.
Wotton-under-Edge Joint Sports Centre. Katherine Lady Berkeley School, Wotton-under-Edge. Tel. (0453) 842626.

All the information given here was correct on publication, but times of opening, etc. are sometimes altered at short notice, so please check before setting off on a grand expedition!

COMMA

77

FAMILY WALKS SERIES

All titles at £3.25

Family Walks in the White Peak. Norman Taylor. ISBN 0 907758 09 6.
"the best Peak District short walks guide yet published." — the Great Outdoors.

Family Walks in the Dark Peak. Norman Taylor. ISBN 0 907758 16 9.
Companion to the first title.

Family Walks in the Cotswolds. Gordon Ottewell. ISBN 0 907758 15 0.

Family Walks around Bristol, Bath and the Mendips. Nigel Vile. ISBN 0 907758 19 3.

Family Walks in Hereford and Worcester. Gordon Ottewell. ISBN 0 907758 20 7.

Family Walks in the Downs and Vales of Wiltshire. Nigel Vile. ISBN 0 907758 21 5.

Family Walks in South Yorkshire. Norman Taylor. ISBN 0 907758 25 8.

Family Walks in the Wye Valley. Heather and Jon Hurley. ISBN 0 907758 26 6.

Family Walks in Mid-Wales. Laurence Main. ISBN 0 907758 27 4.

Family Walks in South Shropshire and the Welsh Borders. Marian Newton.
ISBN 0 907758 30 4.

Family Walks in the Staffordshire Peak and Potteries. Les Lumsdon. ISBN 0 907758 34 7.

Family Walks in Cheshire. Chris Buckland. ISBN 0 907758 29 0.

Family Walks in South Gloucestershire. Gordon Ottewell. ISBN 0 907758 33 9.

Family Walks in Snowdonia. Laurence Main. ISBN 0 907758 32 0.

Ready Spring 1991

Family Walks in North West Kent
Family Walks in Berkshire and North Hampshire
Family Walks the Teme Valley
Family Walks in Sedgemoor, Avalon and Mendip
Family Walks in Oxfordshire

Other titles in preparation.

The Publishers, D. J. Mitchell and E. G. Power, welcome suggestions for further titles in this series; and will be pleased to consider other manuscripts of regional interest from new or established authors.